ANTHROPOLOGICAL PAPERS OF
THE UNIVERSITY OF ARIZONA
NUMBER 19

ROY L. CARLSON

WHITE MOUNTAIN REDWARE

A Pottery Tradition of
East-Central Arizona and
Western New Mexico

THE UNIVERSITY OF ARIZONA PRESS
TUCSON, ARIZONA 1970

THE UNIVERSITY OF ARIZONA PRESS

PREFACE

The following study is a revised version of a doctoral dissertation submitted to the University of Arizona in 1961. Certain revisions are the result of incoporating into the original study material on additional vessels from the collections of the University of Colorado Museum. Numerous people have made this work possible. To Raymond H. Thompson, chairman of my dissertation committee, and to Emil W. Haury, of the Department of Anthropology of the University of Arizona and the Arizona State Museum, I owe especial thanks for guidance in this project. I relied heavily on their long familiarity with the pottery types which form the backbone of this dissertation. Edward P. Dozier, who also served as a member of my dissertation committee, provided valuable advice. Wilma Kaemlein assisted greatly in gathering the material for study. William W. Wasley graciously answered my endless questions concerning the identification of various black-on-white pottery types to which it was necessary for me to refer. Richard B. Woodbury and Nathalie F. S. Woodbury generously allowed me to read and refer to their manuscript on Zuni pottery types. The Woodburys also identified the Heshota Polychrome vessels in the collections. Virginia Nelson typed the final manuscript. My wife, Maureen, contributed in many ways to the completion of this study.

Many institutions have contributed to this work. One debt is to Gila Pueblo which donated its entire archaeological collection to the Arizona State Museum in 1951, and from which the bulk of the data used in this study is drawn; however, without the solid chronological foundation derived from the research at Point of Pines by the Department of Anthropology of the University of Arizona and the Arizona State Museum, which was supported at various times by the Wenner-Gren Foundation for Anthropological Research and the National Science Foundation, these data would have been of much less value. The Arizona State Museum contributed photographic supplies necessary for the project. The Amerind Foundation at Dragoon, the Southwest Archeological Center at Globe, the Museum of Northern Arizona at Flagstaff, and the University of Colorado Museum at Boulder made their collections available to me, and to the management and staff of these organizations I owe a debt of thanks for their cooperation and hospitality.

R. L. C.

CONTENTS

LIST OF ILLUSTRATIONS AND TABLE vi

1. INTRODUCTION 1

2. TYPE DESCRIPTIONS 5

    Puerco Black-on-red 7

    Wingate Black-on-red 11

    Wingate Polychrome 17

    St. Johns Black-on-red 29

    St. Johns Polychrome 31

    Springerville Polychrome 41

    Pinedale Polychrome 47

    Pinedale Black-on-red 53

    Cedar Creek Polychrome 57

    Fourmile Polychrome 65

    Showlow Polychrome 73

    Point of Pines Polychrome 77

    Heshota Polychrome, Heshota Black-on-red, Kwakina Polychrome 82

3. DESIGN STYLES 84

    Holbrook Style 88

    Puerco Style 88

    Wingate Style 89

    Tularosa Style 90

    Pinedale Style 91

    Fourmile Style 94

4. CHANGE AND CONTINUITY IN WHITE MOUNTAIN REDWARE 95

    La Plata Phase 95

    White Mound Phase 95

    Kiatuthlanna Phase 96

    Red Mesa Phase 96

    Wingate Phase 96

    Early Pueblo III 99

    Late Pueblo III 101

    Early Pueblo IV 105

    Late Pueblo IV 114

5. SUMMARY AND CONCLUSIONS 116

    REFERENCES 117

ILLUSTRATIONS

1. Sites and locations referred to in the text 2
2. Bowl and jar shapes 6
3. Distribution of Puerco Black-on-red 8
4. Puerco Black-on-red bowls 10
5. Puerco Black-on-red vessels 12
6. Distribution of Wingate Black-on-red 14
7. Wingate Black-on-red bowls 16
8. Wingate Black-on-red bowls, jars, and dipper 18
9. Distribution of Wingate Polychrome 20
10. Early Wingate Polychrome vessels 22
11. Late Wingate Polychrome vessels 24
12. St. Johns Black-on-red vessels 26
13. St. Johns Black-on-red bowls 28
14. Distribution of St. Johns Polychrome and St. Johns Black-on-red 30
15. St. Johns Polychrome bowls 32
16. Frequent St. Johns Polychrome motifs 34
17. St. Johns Polychrome bowls 36
18. St. Johns Polychrome bowls, jars, and dipper 38
19. St. Johns Polychrome bowls 40
20. St. Johns Polychrome bowls 42
21. St. Johns Polychrome bowls 43
22. Distribution of Springerville polychrome 44
23. Springerville Polychrome bowls and jar 46
24. Distribution of Pinedale Polychrome and Pinedale Black-on-red 48
25. Pinedale Polychrome and Kwakina Polychrome vessels 50
26. Pinedale Polychrome bowls 52
27. Pinedale Black-on-red vessels 54
28. Distribution of Cedar Creek Polychrome 56
29. Cedar Creek Polychrome bowls 58
30. Cedar Creek Polychrome bowls 60
31. Cedar Creek Polychrome bowls, jars, and eccentrics 62
32. Distribution of Fourmile Polychrome 64
33. Fourmile Polychrome bowls 66
34. Fourmile Polychrome bowls 68
35. Fourmile Polychrome bowls 70
36. Fourmile Polychrome bowls and jars 72

37. Fourmile Polychrome bowls and jars 74

38. Distribution of Showlow Polychrome 76

39. Showlow Polychrome vessels 78

40. Point of Pines Polychrome bowls 80

41. Point of Pines Polychrome bowls and jars 81

42. Idealized layout found in White Mountain Redware 86-87

43. Holbrook style 88

44. Puerco style 89

45. Wingate style 90

46. Tularosa style 91

47. Pinedale style 92

48. Fourmile style 92

49. Changes in and developments from scrolls in sequent styles
        of White Mountain Redware 93

50. Puerco Black-on-red bowl 98

51. Wingate Black-on-red pitcher 98

52. Some sequent style changes 100

53. Some changes in and developments from multiple bands 102

54. Some changes and continuities in exterior decoration on bowls 106-107

55. Pinedale style 108

56. Some changes in and developments from frets 110

57. Restored Cedar Creek Polychrome bowl 111

58. Bird figures on Fourmile Polychrome bowls 113

59. Late White Mountain Redware bowls with flower designs 115

TABLE

1. Pottery collections used in this study 4

1. INTRODUCTION

From about A.D. 1000 to 1500 a red-slipped pottery with painted black or black-and-white decoration was manufactured in east-central Arizona and western New Mexico. This elaborately decorated pottery has long been recognized as an important tool for chronological and cultural interpretation in Southwestern archaeology. Although the study of this pottery began with Hough (1903) and Fewkes (1904), it was first used systematically by Spier (1917, 1919) in establishing a chronology. Excellent type descriptions of some of the pottery appeared early in the works of Haury (Haury 1930, Haury and Hargrave 1931), Gladwin and Gladwin (1931), and Kidder and Shepard (1936). In 1937 Colton and Hargrave organized much of this pottery into a taxonomic unit named White Mountain Redware on the basis of similarities in various technological attributes and the geographic proximity of the constituent types. There has been no study of the styles of decoration found on this pottery. These styles are the primary concern of this paper.

A total of 477 whole or restorable vessels from the collections listed in Table 1 were examined. These 477 vessels have been grouped into the following twelve types: (1) Puerco Black-on-red; (2) Wingate Black-on-red; (3) Wingate Polychrome; (4) St. Johns Black-on-red; (5) St. Johns Polychrome; (6) Springerville Polychrome; (7) Pinedale Polychrome; (8) Pinedale Black-on-red; (9) Cedar Creek Polychrome; (10) Fourmile Polychrome; (11) Showlow Polychrome; and (12) Point of Pines Polychrome. Detailed descriptions of these types are included in this study. Several other pottery types are part of the White Mountain Redware tradition, but there were insufficient data available for detailed descriptions. In this category are Fourmile Black-on-red, Heshota Polychrome, Heshota Black-on-red, Kwakina Polychrome, and Glaze I Red.

These types of redware constitute a tradition, that is, a socially transmitted developmental continuum through time (Thompson 1956: 39). Traditions themselves may involve the history of either one culture trait or a complex of culture traits; they can be arbitrarily defined providing that the segments of the tradition exhibit spatial contiguity and temporal continuity. The White Mountain Redware tradition,

an arbitrary division of the Cibola painted pottery tradition, is composed of those vessels which have a red slip and painted decoration in either black or black and white, which when grouped into pottery types have a geographic locus within or immediately adjacent to the Cibola area, and which share a number of other attributes indicative of close historical relationships. This tradition is arbitrary in that types of black-on-white pottery which are as closely related historically to redware types as the redware types are to each other are excluded by definition. There are several reasons for this. First and foremost, color pattern has long been the single attribute used in the Southwest in the initial breakdown of any collection of painted pottery into types. Secondary and tertiary divisions can be made, if desired, using any one of a number of other criteria *after* the initial division by color pattern. While this method has certain drawbacks, it does emphasize the widespread changes in color patterns which have broad chronological significance. The second reason for isolating White Mountain Redware is that it provides a convenient unit for analysis and shows that there is a tradition of red pottery with black or black-and-white decoration which can be used as a core to which developments in pottery with other color schemes can be related.

The word "ware" is not used in the taxonomic sense of Colton (1953), but simply means a group of pottery types which share many of the same attributes.

Chronological and distributional data indicate that there are three regions in which variants of the White Mountain Redware tradition are found: (1) *Cibola* which is defined as the area from approximately Tohatchi, New Mexico on the north to Carrizo Wash on the south, and from the continental divide on the east to the Petrified Forest on the west. This area is partly Mogollon and partly Anasazi in its early culture history, but by the time of the appearance of White Mountain Redware about A.D. 1000, it is typically Anasazi. It should be noted that this area differs from what Wheat (1955) and Danson (1957) would include in the Cibola branch of the Mogollon. The Zuni Indians occupied part of this area historically. The pottery types which center in this area are

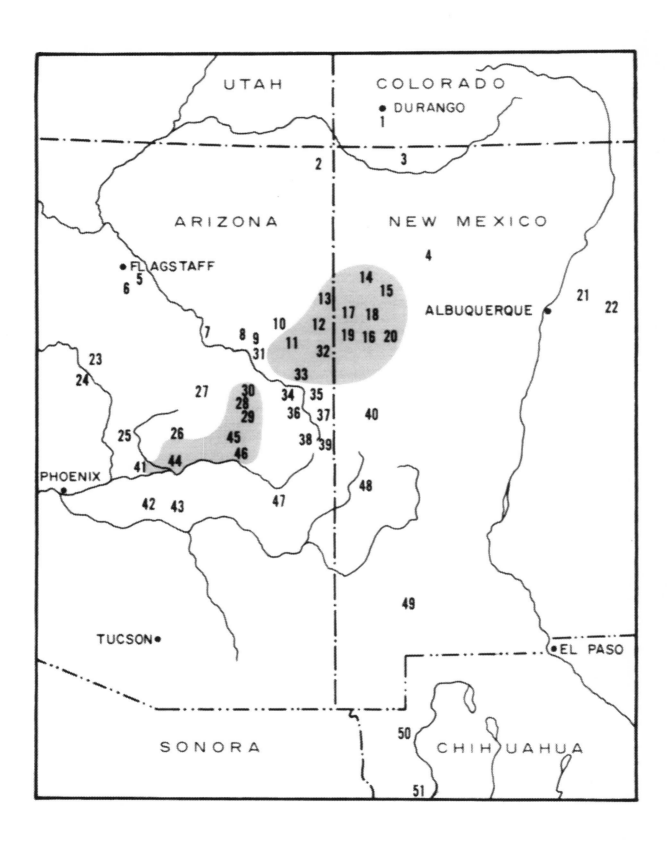

Puerco Black-on-red, Wingate Black-on-red, Wingate Polychrome, St. Johns Polychrome, St. Johns Black-on-red, Heshota Polychrome, Heshota Black-on-red, and Kwakina Polychrome. (2) *Mogollon Rim* which is defined as lying from Roosevelt Lake on the west to the White River on the east, and from the southern reaches of the Silver Creek drainage on the north to the Salt River on the south. The early culture history of this area, up to Pueblo III, is largely Mogollon and only later Anasazi. In historic times it was occupied only by the wandering Apache. Pottery types indigenous to this area are Pinedale Polychrome, Pinedale Black-on-red, Cedar Creek Polychrome, Fourmile Polychrome, Fourmile Black-on-red, and Showlow Polychrome. It is quite likely that St. Johns Polychrome was also manufactured in this area, but this cannot be demonstrated satisfactorily at the present. (3) *Rio Grande* valley. This area has produced a regional variant not specifically part of this study, but

nevertheless worthy of mention. Mera (1935) suggested originally that the Rio Grande Glaze I Red developed out of late St. Johns Polychrome in the Rio Grande valley, and Stubbs and Stallings (1953, Fig. 70) see a continuity from this early glazed type into the historic wares of Zia and Santa Ana. Glaze I Red belongs stylistically to the same horizon as Pinedale Polychrome, Pinedale Black-on-red, and Heshota Polychrome and it is certainly related, to a degree, to these types. All three regional variants are sections of a diverging tradition. Although St. Johns Polychrome and St. Johns Black-on-red belong primarily to the Cibola section, it is from them that later types in the other areas diverged.

Two pottery types, Springerville Polychrome and Point of Pines Polychrome, have not been relegated to any of the foregoing regional variants. Springerville Polychrome seems to belong to the region of roughly the upper Little Colorado River between the Cibola

---

FIG. 1. Sites and locations referred to in the text. *Shaded areas:* Upper, Cibola area; Lower, Mogollon Rim area.

1. Mesa Verde
2. Vandal Cave
3. Aztec National Monument
4. Chaco Canyon National Monument
5. Wupatki National Monument
6. Turkey Hill Pueblo
7. Homolovi
8. Tusayan 16:1, 16:2, and 16:3
9. Ft. Defiance 13:1 and 13:4
10. White Mound
11. Ft. Defiance 15:1 and 15:5
12. Whitewater district, Allentown ruins
13. Lupton area sites
14. Pipeline survey sites; LA 2508, 2655, 2700, 2701, 2699, 2640, 2639
15. Red Mesa sites
16. Wingate 14:1 and 14:2
17. Wingate 9:8
18. Village of the Great Kivas and Nutri Canyon
19. Zuni
20. El Morro (Atsinna)
21. Pindi Pueblo
22. Pecos Pueblo
23. Verde 5:11
24. Verde 5:41
25. Verde 15:30, Rye Creek Ruin
26. Holbrook 13:6
27. Heber region
28. Pinedale Ruin, Holbrook 12:11
29. Showlow Ruin, Holbrook 12:2
30. Fourmile Ruin, Holbrook 12:3
31. Petrified Forest
32. St. Johns 4:1
33. Kiatuthlanna
34. St. Johns 6:1
35. St. Johns 7:1 and 7:2
36. St. Johns 10:1
37. St. Johns 12:1
38. Greer, Eagar, and Springerville
39. St. Johns 16:1, 16:2, and 16:15
40. Quemado
41. Sites around Roosevelt Lake: Roosevelt 3:3, 5:5, 5:8, 5:10, 5:11, 6:2, 6:3, 6:4, 9:5, 9:8, and 9:20
42. Florence 3:11
43. Globe 6:1, Gila Pueblo
44. Ariz. C:2:8, Canyon Creek Ruin, Cherry Creek
45. Forestdale
46. Kinishba
47. Point of Pines
48. Pine Lawn Valley
49. Mimbres Valley
50. Chihuahua A:16:2
51. Casas Grandes

and Mogollon Rim areas. This region is actually little known and much of the redware from there intergrades with temporally equivalent pottery types of the other areas. Point of Pines Polychrome, which is found only at Point of Pines, appears to be the product of a pueblo group that previously manufactured very little painted redware. As such, it could be classed as a fourth, though minor, regional variant of White Mountain Redware.

Type descriptions, a breakdown of the six major styles found on the ware, and a summary of the history of White Mountain Redware are presented in the following sections of this report.

TABLE 1

POTTERY COLLECTIONS USED IN THIS STUDY

COLLECTIONS	Puerco Black-on-red	Wingate Black-on-red	Wingate Poly.	St. Johns Black-on-red	St. Johns Poly.	Springerville Poly.	Pinedale Poly.	Pinedale Black-on-red	Cedar Creek Poly.	Fourmile Poly.	Showlow Poly.	Point of Pines Poly.
ARIZONA STATE MUSEUM												
Gila Pueblo	26	32	15	20	70	8	14	11	13	48	3	· ·
Point of Pines	· ·	6	4	7	8	1	9	7	19	12	1	15
Kinishba	· ·	· ·	· ·	· ·	· ·	· ·	7	· ·	4	17	4	· ·
Other	· ·	2	2	1	6	· ·	3	1	1	7	· ·	· ·
SOUTHWEST ARCHEOLOGICAL CENTER	3	1	1	1	7	1	· ·	3	1	1	· ·	· ·
AMERIND FOUNDATION	· ·	4	· ·	· ·	1	· ·	1	3	1	4	· ·	1
MUSEUM OF NORTHERN ARIZONA	1	5	· ·	3	4	· ·	1	· ·	1	3	· ·	· ·
UNIVERSITY OF COLORADO MUSEUM	2	4	4	3	4	· ·	1	1	· ·	2	· ·	· ·
TOTAL	32	54	26	35	100	10	36	26	40	94	8	16

2. TYPE DESCRIPTIONS

The pottery is grouped into types according to standard Southwestern taxonomy (Gifford 1953) although the categories used do not specifically follow any pre-existing system. The major division into black-on-reds and polychromes is essentially a descriptive one, but within these two categories attribute clusters are characteristic of each type. In order to be useful a pottery type should ideally (1) exhibit attributes or clusters of attributes peculiar to itself alone, (2) be capable of being recognized in both sherd and whole vessel form, and (3) be meaningful in terms of a specific time period in a given area. Types are considered to have both modal attributes and a range of attributes outside the mode. The modal attributes differentiate one type from another whereas the less frequent attributes either grade into other types temporally or spatially, or they are idiosyncratic. The pottery types described in this study have been formulated with these criteria in mind. Many of the descriptions are basically the same as previous ones; others are markedly different.

A number of the types will prove, I think, to be capable of further subdivision into "regional varieties" as our knowledge of them increases. Certain suggestions along these lines are made in the discussion section following some of the type descriptions. A regional variety differs from what Wheat, Gifford, and Wasley (1958: 36) term a variety in that it is recognized by the clustering of minor attributes in a localized geographic area within the area of distribution of the type as a whole. Whereas one regional variety of a type may or may not have a slightly greater or lesser temporal range than other varieties of the same type, the basis for division must be geographic, not temporal. A good example of a regional variety is Vivian's (1959: 26-8) identification of what can best be called a Chaco Variety of McElmo Black-on-white. Wheat, Gifford, and Wasley (1958: 36) speak of three aspects of a variety: (1) technological or stylistic, (2) areal, (3) temporal. They consider any one of these aspects a basis for a variety. The difficulty I find with this method of classification is that the aspects are given equal weight in differentiating a variety, but they are not mutually exclusive. Using various criteria which are not mutually exclusive as a basis for subdivision makes it potentially necessary to formulate varieties of varieties in instances where either diagnostic attributes of two or more varieties of a type are found on the same sherd or vessel, or in cases where recognizable regional variations of what was previously defined as a variety occur. Such usage could lead to taxonomic bedlam. My contention is that one criterion should be used as a basis for establishing varieties, and this basis should be the occurrence of minor attributes which cluster in a local geographic area within the area of distribution of the type as a whole. I also contend that widespread technological or stylistic variations which are not geographically meaningful are best described either within the range of variation of the type as a whole, or used as the basis for a separate type depending on the usefulness of the category. In addition, I also think that this is the only way in which the variety concept can adequately function for the purpose for which it was intended, that is, to show the relationships of horizontally related ceramic units without increasing the plethora of type names.

Most of the categories in the type descriptions are self-explanatory, but some comments are necessary. Color references are based on the Munsell Soil Color Chart. Idealized examples of bowl and jar shapes are shown in Figure 2. Sub-groups of bowls are differentiated on the basis of the curvature of the wall and the depth-diameter ratio. Medium depth bowls are those whose maximum diameters are between two and three times their maximum height; deep bowls are those whose maximum diameters are less than twice their maximum height. The other shapes are self-explanatory. The styles of decoration on bowl interiors and jar exteriors are described in Chapter 3 of this report. The spatial distributions of types were worked out from the Gila Pueblo survey sherd boards in the Arizona State Museum. The center of distribution was determined by enclosing the area which contained sites with the type in quantity. The periphery of the distribution was determined by the distribution of the sherds on the boards, by plotting the location of whole vessels, and by references in the archaeological literature to definite occurrences of the type. Since neither Pinedale Black-on-red nor St. Johns Black-on-red could be satisfactorily distinguished from their respective polychromes using the

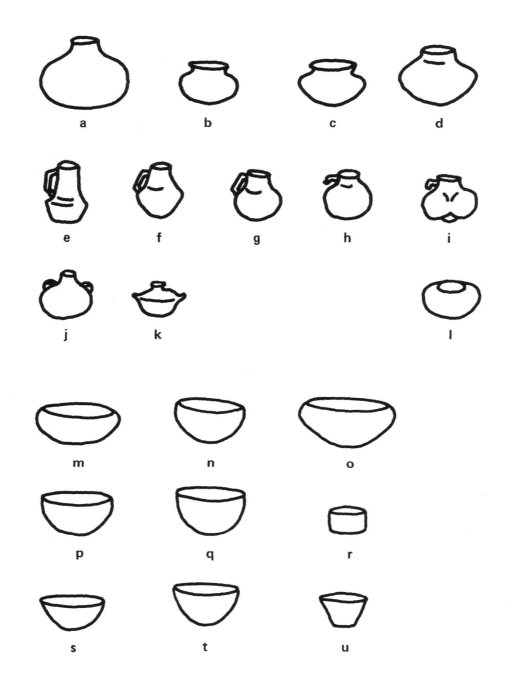

FIG. 2. Bowl and jar shapes.
a-d. Simple necked jars
e-i. Pitchers
j,k. Canteens
l. Neckless jar or "seed jar"
m-o. Bowls with incurved rims

p,q. Bowls whose walls become vertical just below the rim
r. Bowl with vertical sides and flat base or "paint cup"
s,t. Bowls with flaring sides
u. "Flower pot"

small sherds on these boards, the distributions were combined. Temporal distributions are based on tree-ring dates where possible; otherwise they are inferred from other data.

PUERCO BLACK-ON-RED

History

Named by: Gladwin and Gladwin 1934, Fig. 4.

Synonyms: Black-on-red found at Chaco, in part (Hawley 1950: 47); North Plains Black-on-red, in part (Olson and Wasley 1956, Fig. 234 *G*); Little Colorado ware, in part (Roberts 1932: 110).

Previous descriptions: Colton and Hargrave 1937: 120-1; Martin and Willis 1940, Pl. 74; Hawley 1950: 47; Olson and Wasley 1956: 303; Vivian 1959: 31.

Type sites: Fort Defiance 15: 4 (Gladwin and Gladwin 1934); NA 933, Cottonwood Seep, Puerco River, Navajo County, Arizona (Colton and Hargrave 1937: 120).

Basis of present description: Analysis of 32 whole or restorable vessels; reference to previous descriptions where specified.

Technology

Construction: Coiling followed by scraping.

Paste: Usually light brown to orange, occasionally white to light gray; inclusions are white, gray, red, or black angular fragments of which at least some are sherds; rounded quartz particles are sometimes present also; a carbon streak is present in some cases.

Wall thickness: 4 to 7 mm., usually 5 to 6 mm.

Paint: The black paint appears to be iron or an iron-carbon mixture. Hawley (1950: 47) describes it as "thin black iron paint applied after polishing." The paint on these vessels is more variable than this, but whatever its constituents it penetrates into the slip.

Surface finish: Bowls are slipped red on the interior and exterior; jars are slipped in the same manner on the exterior and, with one exception, on the interior of the neck. Bowl interiors vary from very smooth to bumpy; exteriors are usually uneven and poorly polished. Temper particles sometimes protrude through the slip. The slip varies in thickness and is frequently powdery and weathered looking. Small or large fire clouds occur on the exterior of most vessels.

Slip color: Red, usually 10R 4/6 or 10R 5/6, occasionally 10R 5/8 or 10R 5/4 or intermediate grades.

Shapes

Bowls: Six shapes are present; all have rounded bases: (1) medium depth with flaring sides - 15 examples; dia. 22.0 - 29.0 cm.; ht. 9.0 - 12.8 cm.; (2) medium depth with sides that become vertical at the rim - 4 examples; dia. 20.2 - 24.6 cm.; ht. 8.0 - 10.3 cm.; (3) deep with flaring sides - 1 example; dia. 22.9 cm.; ht. 12.0 cm.; (4) deep with sides that become vertical at the rim - 1 example; dia. 23.0 cm.; ht. 12.2 cm.; (5) medium depth with walls that incurve at the rim - 1 example; dia. 20.4 cm.; ht. 9.6 cm.; incurvature 2 mm.; and (6) deep with walls that incurve at the rim - 1 example; dia. 19.3 cm.; ht. 10.5 cm.; incurvature 2.5 mm. Rims are flattened or slightly rounded with no bevel or lip. In a few instances the wall is thinned at the rim.

Jars: Five jar shapes are present: (1) pitchers with long globular bodies, middle or high rounded shoulders, and strap handles - 4 examples; dia. 12.0 - 17.0 cm.; ht. 16.0 - 19.0 cm.; (2) a canteen with a squat globular body, relatively long constricted neck, and a pair of strap handles which have been ground off flush with the surface of the vessel - 1 example; dia. 15.6 cm.; ht. 14.5 cm.; (3) pitcher with broken lug handle and medium length neck - 1 example; ht. 9.4 cm.; dia. 10.7 cm.; and (4) simple jar - 1 example; ht. 9.4 cm.; dia. 10.7 cm.

Dippers: One example with a hollow handle; diameter of bowl, 10.8 cm.

Effigies: One example of a bilobate based, long-necked jar with a strap handle; the lobes form a dog's body on which the head rests; dia. 11.5 cm.; ht. 11.5 cm.

Painted Decoration

Fields of decoration: Bowl and dipper interiors, jar exteriors, effigy exteriors, and sometimes rims and handles bear painted motifs. Jar necks and bodies are treated as one field. Bowl exteriors are not decorated although one vessel (Fig. 4 *g*) bears three small black dashes.

Color patterns: All bowls are black-on-red on the interior and red on the exterior. All jars are black-on-red on the exterior.

Banding lines: On four vessels there is no upper banding line and the rim itself serves as the upper edge of the band. On the remaining vessels the banding lines are the same width as either the hatching or the frets.

Line and motif width: Hatching lines vary from 1 to 3 mm. in width, but are most frequently 3 mm.

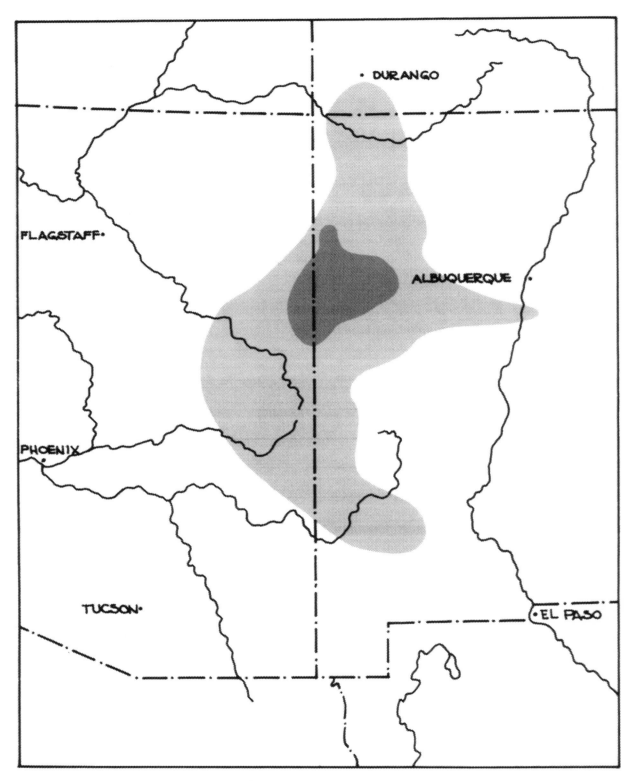

FIG. 3. Distribution of Puerco Black-on-red. Light area shows limit of distribution; dark area shows greatest concentration.

The uncomplicated portions of frets vary from 3 to 6 mm. in width, but are almost always 5 mm. The outer line of parallel-hatched motifs or panel dividers is the same width as the internal hatching lines.

Style: Fourteen vessels are decorated in typical Holbrook style. There is one other vessel which departs from this style only in that the decoration focuses on the whole interior of the bowl. Fifteen vessels are decorated in typical Puerco style; four others are basically in this style but show attributes transitional to Wingate style.

Other Features

Rim notching: Rim notching in the form of four opposed notches neatly ground into the rim occurs on one bowl (Fig. 4 *i*).

Spatial Distribution

The distribution of Puerco Black-on-red is illustrated in Figure 3. The type is found from Mesa Verde on the north, east to the Rio Grande, south to the Mimbres valley in New Mexico, and west to the vicinity of Pinedale, Arizona. It occurs at 162 sites of the Gila Pueblo survey within this area. The distribution of Puerco Black-on-red centers between the upper Puerco River and the headwaters of the San Jose where it is not only more frequent in sites, but where there are more sites which contain it. It is much more common in sites north of this central area than in sites to the south or west. Sites in Chaco Canyon and Aztec national monuments show a high percentage of Puerco Black-on-red sherds.

Temporal Distribution

Puerco Black-on-red has appeared at a number of dated archaeological sites. Roberts illustrates seven vessels from the Village of the Great Kivas (1932, Figs. 28 *a, b,* 29 *a,* 35 *b, c*). The date for this site is given at A.D. 1015 ± 15 years (Roberts 1932: 156). This date, however, seems much too early for the pottery complex of the site as a whole, at least as far as the types associated with the burials are concerned. Kidder (Kidder and Shepard 1936: 353) has previously questioned this date, but on different grounds. Dutton (1939, Tables 2, 22) reports two incomplete vessels from Leyit Kin in Chaco Canyon, one of which, from Room 16, Unit III, was found in association with materials dating between approximately A.D. 1050 and 1150. Two of the vessels used in this study were found in the fill of Room 41 at Kin

Kletso, associated with McElmo, Gallup, and Escavada Black-on-whites. Vivian (1959: 31, 68) reports some Puerco Black-on-red sherds from the earliest level at the Hubbard Site in Aztec National Monument. The earliest level at this Site has a tree-ring date of A.D. 1109 and is assigned to the McElmo Phase, A.D. 1050–1150. Sherds were found in the Montezuma Phase at the Hubbard Site, as well as in the early Montezuma Phase at LA 2520 near Aztec, which has a suggested date of A.D. 1150 to 1200 (Cassidy 1956: 21). The materials associated with Puerco Black-on-red at the Village of the Great Kivas suggest that this type is contemporaneous with Wingate Polychrome which appears to have lasted until about A.D. 1200. The latter type as well as early St. Johns Polychrome and Pinedale Polychrome occasionally exhibit the style of interior design found on Puerco Black-on-red vessels (Figs. 15 *a, i,* 25 *c*). Some of the vessels included in this study come from the Reserve and Tularosa phases at Point of Pines and the Reserve area of New Mexico. These phases lack tree-ring dates, but the Reserve Phase is generally thought to have begun about A.D. 1000 (Martin and Rinaldo 1950: 557; Breternitz 1959: 71). At the Cerro Colorado Site near Quemado, Puerco Black-on-red occurs in Ceramic Period E with a suggested date of A.D. 1000 to 1100. Stubbs and Stallings (1953: 14, 156) report both Puerco Black-on-red and Wingate Black-on-red from the pre-Pindi horizon at Pindi Pueblo which has tree-ring dates of about A.D. 1215. This, however, seems somewhat late for these types. The most reasonable temporal limits for the type seem to be A.D. 1000 to 1200 with the highest frequency of occurrence toward the middle of the period.

Discussion

When Gladwin and Gladwin (1934, Fig. 4) first used the name Puerco Black-on-red, they were undoubtedly referring to the same vessels from the Gila Pueblo collections which have been used in the present type description, although they never described them. In 1936 Hawley coupled the name to a description which was accepted by Colton and Hargrave (1937) and Martin and Willis (1940). Later, however, the type was referred to as an "enigmatic creation of archaeologists" (Wasley 1959: 220), a view concurred in by many. It is probable that Puerco Black-on-red is a valid type. In general, the name has been used to classify sherds which resemble Wingate

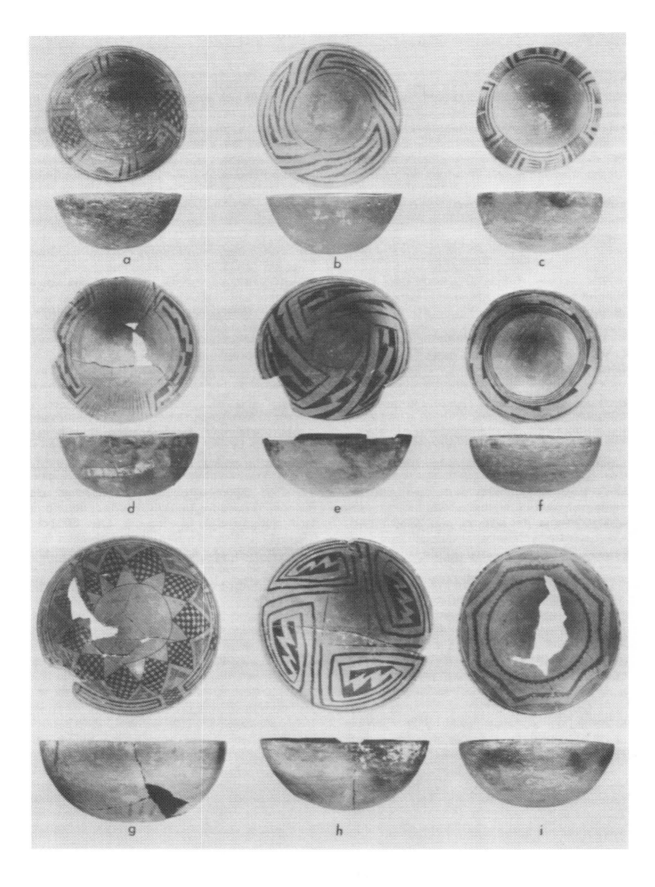

a   b   c

d   e   f

g   h   i

Black-on-red, but which show solid linear motifs and little or no hatching. Its definition as a type is based for the most part on a good correlation of open bowls with flaring sides with decoration consisting of either solid or solid and parallel-hatched, non-interlocked design units. This correlation has been extended, on the basis of design, to jars and to bowls outside the modal shape.

Typologically, Puerco Black-on-red is the earliest type among the White Mountain Redwares, although this cannot be documented stratigraphically with reference to Wingate Black-on-red which occupies much of the same time period.

Regional varieties may someday be recognized, but in the present sample neither the vessels with orange-brown nor those with gray-white paste were clustered in mutually exclusive areas. The same may be said for the two main styles—Puerco and Holbrook—although I would suspect that Holbrook style concentrates more to the west within the area of distribution. It is possible that Puerco Black-on-red was made in the Chaco since Hawley (1934) notes the presence of the requisite clays there.

Summary Description

Puerco Black-on-red pots are slipped red on the interior and exterior of bowls, and on the exterior of jars. The paste is light brown to white with sherd and quartz sand temper. The paint, either a faded brown or a good black, penetrates the slip. The most typical shapes are bowls with flaring sides and rounded bases, and pitchers with long necks. Bowl exteriors are never decorated. Decoration goes to the rim and consists of medium-width solid motifs, usually frets, which often have barbed ends and sometimes pendant dots. Parallel-hatched motifs, which consist of either panel dividers or encircling bands, are common. Layouts are usually banded and frequently sectioned vertically with checkerboards or parallel-hatched dividers. Inter-

locked solid and hatched motifs do not occur. The distribution is primarily north-south along the Arizona-New Mexico border from Mesa Verde to the Mimbres valley. The area of most common occurrence is the Puerco River valley and its immediate vicinity. The estimated time range is A.D. 1000 to 1200 with the most certain dating being toward the middle of this period.

WINGATE BLACK-ON-RED

History

Named by: Gladwin and Gladwin 1931: 29.
Synonyms: Two color painted ware (Spier 1919, Table 1); Little Colorado Black-on-red ware (Hawley 1929: 734); Little Colorado ware, in part (Roberts 1932: 110); North Plains black-on-red, in part (Olson and Wasley 1956: 303).
Previous descriptions: Gladwin and Gladwin 1931: 2; Colton and Hargrave 1937: 120; Martin and Willis 1940, Pl. 95 6; Hawley 1950: 48; Olson and Wasley 1956: 303.
Type site: St. Johns 11: 1 (Gladwin and Gladwin 1931).
Basis of present description: Analysis of 54 whole or restorable vessels; reference to previous descriptions where specified.

Technology

Construction: Coiling followed by scraping.
Paste: White to gray, buff, or pink. A carbon streak is frequently present. Inclusions are white, buff, red, or black angular fragments, most of which are sherds. Rounded quartz particles are sometimes present.
Wall thickness: 4 to 7 mm., usually 5 to 6 mm.
Paint: Hawley (1950: 48) describes the black paint as an iron and carbon mixture. The edges of the

FIG. 4.   Puerco Black-on-red bowls.
  a. GP-02409. St. Johns 4:1.
  b. GP-01614. Ft. Defiance 15:1.
  c. GP-02541. St. Johns 4:1.
  d. GP-01604. Ft. Defiance 15:1.
  e. GP-02413. St. Johns 4:1.
  f. GP-02977. Tusayan 16:3.
  g. GP-51607. New Mexico F:14:1, Burial 50.

  h. GP-02640. St. Johns 4:1.
  i. GP-01094. Tusayan 16:1.
  a, c, d, and f are good Puerco style; g and i are basically Puerco style but show attributes transitional to Wingate and Tularosa styles.
  Diameter of g is 29 cm.

painted lines vary from sharp to slightly fuzzy. In appearance the paint varies from a thin brownish stain to a good black.

Surface finish: Bowls and dippers are slipped on the interior and exterior with a thick red slip. Jars and eccentrics are slipped in the same manner on the exterior. Necked jars are slipped on the interior of the neck. The interiors of bowls and the exteriors of jars are polished. In some instances the polishing appears to go over the black painted designs. Though polished, these surfaces are usually not well smoothed, and sometimes show pitting over the temper. On bowl exteriors the thick slip is bumpy and uneven although it does show wide polishing marks. The slip wears off easily and frequently appears powdery and mat finished. A small amount of crazing is present on many vessels. Small or large fire clouds appear on the exteriors of most vessels.

Slip color: Red: Munsell 10R 5/6, 26 vessels; 10R 4/6, 22 vessels; 7.5R 4/6, 1 vessel; 10R 5/8, 1 vessel; 10R 4/8, 1 vessel; or weak red 10R 5/5, 3 vessels. Color illustrations may be found in Roberts (1932, Pl. 27 *d, e*), Gladwin and Gladwin (1931, Pl. 32), and Hough (1903, Pl. 36).

Shapes

Bowls: All bowls have rounded bottoms. There are five shapes present on the basis of depth and wall form: (1) medium depth with incurved rims - 9 examples; dia. 20.6 - 33.3 cm.; ht. 9.9 - 14.0 cm.; incurvature 1 - 3.5 mm; (2) deep with incurved rims - 3 examples; dia. 23.0 - 31.5 cm.; ht. 12.0 - 15.8 cm.; incurvature 1.5 - 7 mm.; (3) medium depth with sides which become vertical just below the rim - 18 examples; dia. 17.2 - 35.8 cm.; ht. 9.3 - 17.7 cm.; (4) medium depth with flaring sides - 7 examples; dia. 20.8 - 33.8 cm.; ht. 9.0 - 15.0 cm.; and (5) deep with flaring sides - 2 examples; dia. 24.1 - 27.5 cm.; ht.

13.4 - 14.8 cm. Bowl rims are flattened to slightly rounded on the top - 34 examples, or internally beveled with a slight external lip - 5 examples. One of the former shows internal thickening at the rim. The latter are probably late in the type.

Jars: There are five jar forms present: (1) pitchers with long necks, high sharp or rounded shoulders, flat or rounded bases, and strap handles - 5 examples; dia. 13.0 - 15.2 cm.; ht. 16.0 - 19.4 cm.; handles are curved or rectanguloid in outline and are joined to the neck or to the neck and shoulders; on two vessels the handle is shaped like a small burden basket (Fig. 8 *a, b*); (2) pitchers with medium length necks, strap handles, and rounded shoulders, bodies, and bases - 3 examples; dia. 12.7 - 16.6 cm.; ht. 14.6 - 16.0 cm.; strap handles are S-shaped in outline, and are attached to the neck and body; (3) jars with no handles, medium length necks, and rounded bodies, bases, and shoulders - 1 example; dia. 18.2 cm.; ht. 16.6 cm.; (4) seed jar - 1 example; dia. 17.5 cm.; ht. 12.0 cm.; and (5) a canteen with a narrow neck, high sharp shoulders, perforated lug handles, and a flattened base - one specimen; dia. 13.3 cm.; ht. 9.3 cm.; Martin and Willis (1940, Pl. 94 *11*) illustrate a Wingate canteen with rounded shoulders. They also show a sixth jar form (Pl. 94 *9*), a pitcher with a trilobate body, short neck, and effigy lug handle.

Dippers: Two specimens, each with an oval bowl; the handle from one is missing, the other is hollow with a perforated end; length, 26 cm.; width, 11.9 - 14 cm.

Eccentrics: Two miniatures, a canteen and a pitcher. Martin and Willis (1940, Pl. 94 *2*) illustrate a Wingate Black-on-red ring vessel.

Painted Decoration

Fields of decoration: Bowl and dipper interiors, jar necks, and jar bodies. Sometimes rims, handles,

---

FIG. 5. Puerco Black-on-red vessels.
- *a.* GP-05981. Wingate 14:1.
- *b.* GP-02117. Ft. Defiance 13:1.
- *c.* GP-01717. Ft. Defiance 15:1.
- *d.* GP-03302. St. Johns 11:1.
- *e.* GP-05983. Wingate 14:1.
- *f.* GP-01949. St. Johns 7:2.
- *g.* GP-02970. Tusayan 16:3.
- *h.* GP-01946. St. Johns 7:2.
- *i.* GP-03386. Provenience unknown.
- *j.* GP-02540. St. Johns 7:2.

- *k.* GP-05973. Wingate 14:2.
- *l.* GP-02543. St. Johns 4:1.
- *m.* GP-05558. Provenience unknown.
- *n.* GP-01298. Tusayan 16:2.

a-c, e, f, i, j, and *l* are Puerco style: *d, g, h, k, m,* and *n* are Holbrook style. The central figure in *b* and the whole field focus of decoration in *m* are atypical.

Diameter of *n* is 24.8 cm.

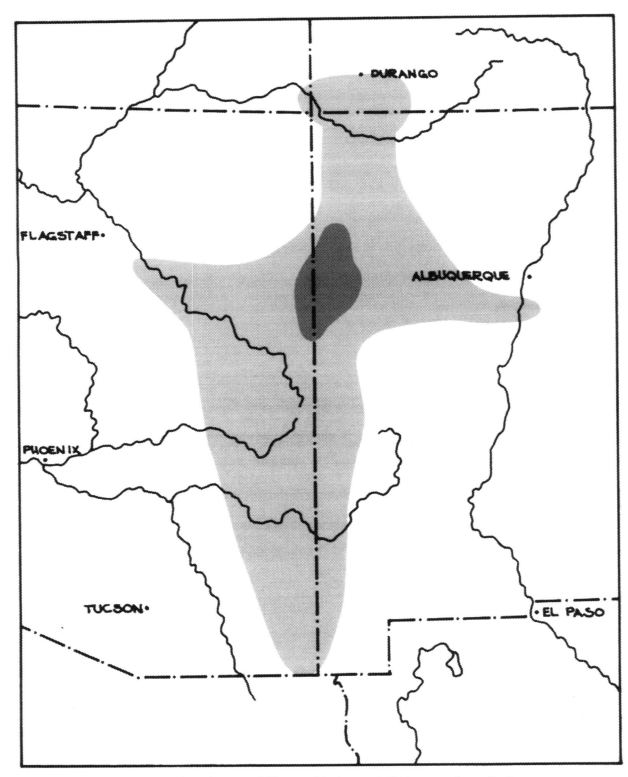

FIG. 6. Distribution of Wingate Black-on-red. Light area shows limit of distribution; dark area shows greatest concentration.

and jar exteriors act as one field. In one instance a bowl exterior was used.

Color patterns: All bowls are black-on-red on the interior and red on the exterior with the exception of an occasional small black design unit. All jars are black-on-red on the exterior. Dippers are black-on-red on the bowl interior, and black-on-red on the handle. Bowl exteriors are not usually decorated; however, one bowl (Fig. 8 *m*) exhibits a continuous band of non-interlocked pendant scrolls on the exterior wall. The design is done in slip paint. The background of roughened slip paint is approximately the same color red. Roberts (1932, Fig. 31) illustrates some small, narrow line, unit motifs from exteriors of black-on-red bowls. He likens these unit motifs—single spirals, triangles, hourglass figures, frets—to ownership marks. An angled line on one of the bowls in this collection (Fig. 7 *e*) may represent such a unit.

Banding lines: None of the vessels with central figured motifs has a banding line around the rim of the bowl or the base of the jar. The upper banding line is also absent on three bowls with banded layouts. No vessels with a double banding line were found in this collection, although Martin and Willis (1940, Pls. 92 *6*, 93 *1*) illustrate two bowls with double framing lines. On one of these the framing line shows a break. These bowls, however, may be St. Johns Black-on-red.

Line and motif width: Framing lines are the same size as hatching lines. They range from 1 to 2 mm. in width, although most are closest to 1 mm. The uncomplicated portions of solid linear motifs range from 3 to 9 mm. in width, averaging 5 mm. The uncomplicated portions of hatched motifs are from 10 to 25 mm. wide, averaging 18 mm.

Style: Forty-two vessels are decorated in good Wingate style. One pitcher (Fig. 8 *e*) is Wingate style on the neck and Puerco style on the body. Roberts (1931, Pl. 16 *a*) illustrates a pitcher which is Wingate style on the neck and Holbrook style on the body. Another pitcher (Fig. 8 *f*) that bears no hatched decoration and does not conform to any of the styles in this study, differs only in that the normally hatched areas are painted solid. Another pitcher (Fig. 8 *b*) is closer to Dogoszhi style, but has both solid and hatched units. One canteen (Fig. 8 *o*) could possibly have been classified as Puerco Black-on-red on a stylistic basis. Seven vessels which are stylistically closer to Tularosa than to Wingate style could possibly have been classified as St. Johns Black-on-

red, although the slip color and characteristics are more like those of Wingate Black-on-red. One bowl (Fig. 7 *b*) shows vertically hatched panel dividers as in Puerco style; otherwise it is good Wingate style.

Other Features

Rim notching: One dipper (Fig. 8 *1*) has four opposed notches in the rim. They are not carefully made, but they appear to be intentional. This dipper is from east of Greer, Arizona, near Mt. Baldy.

Spatial Distribution

The distribution of Wingate Black-on-red is shown in Figure 6. It is about the same as that for Puerco Black-on-red except for being a little more widespread in almost every direction. Roughly, the distribution is from near Monument Ruin, Utah, on the north, east to approximately the junction of the San Jose and the Puerco River, south to the Mexican border, and west to Wupatki National Monument. The Gila Pueblo survey records 202 sites containing Wingate Black-on-red within this area. The core area is the same as for Puerco Black-on-red with the center in the Cibola region. There are 87 recorded sites with this type within the core area. The greatest concentration of these sites is within an area about 200 miles in any direction from where the Puerco River crosses the Arizona-New Mexico border. The frequency of occurrence is very much higher to the north of the core area than to the south. It is relatively common at Chaco and Aztec national monuments. The distribution is very thin west of the Little Colorado River and south of the Gila River.

Temporal Distribution

Various tree-ring dates have been published for sites containing Wingate Black-on-red. These range from about A.D. 850, which is not a bark date (Gladwin 1945: 75), to much later dates (Smiley, Stubbs, and Bannister 1953). The most significant dates include a bark date of A.D. 1047 obtained by Wendorf (1956: 193) from a structure at LA 2505 at the southern end of the Chaco drainage which contained small amounts of Wingate Black-on-red, and bark dates clustering at A.D. 1123 and 1118 obtained by Wasley from Arizona K:12:6 and K:12:5 along the Puerco River near Lupton, Arizona. These sites contained Wingate Black-on-red, but in very limited quantities. Arizona K:12:5 also yielded reused beams with dates approximately 100 years

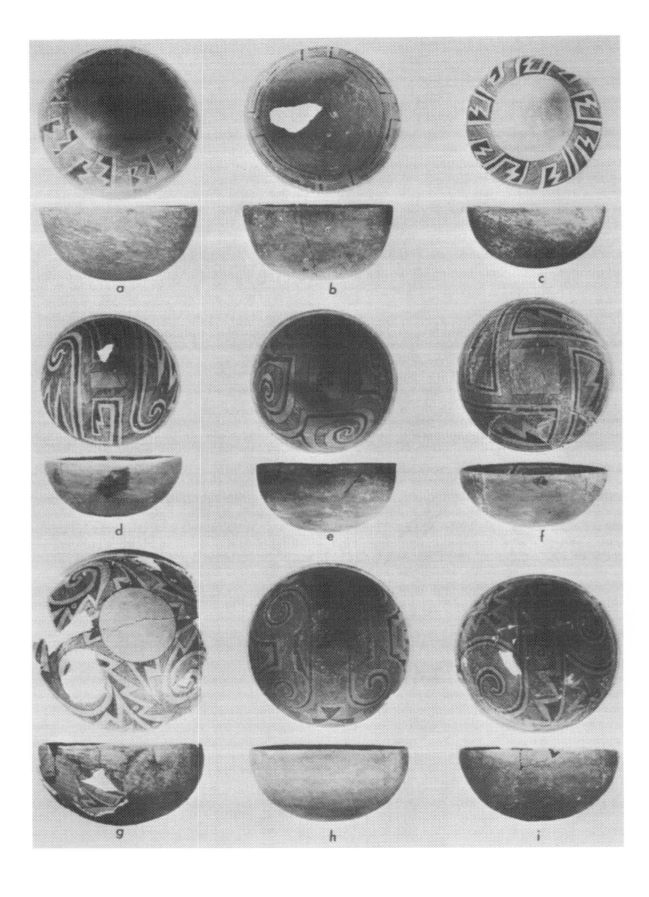

a   b   c

d   e   f

g   h   i

earlier. These data suggest that Wingate Black-on-red was being made as early as A.D. 1047, but did not appear in quantity until after A.D. 1123. A total time range from about A.D. 1050 to 1200 does not seem out of line for this type. The distribution certainly indicates that Wingate Black-on-red belongs to early Pueblo III, that is, to the time period at and just before the abandonment of the Chaco and adjacent parts of the San Juan area.

Discussion

The original type description of Wingate Black-on-red was made by the Gladwins (1931: 29-31) who defined it on the basis of a maroon color. This, to me, seems applicable only to some of those specimens which are worn or weathered and appear closest to 10R 4/6 on the Munsell Soil Color Chart. Olson and Wasley (1956: 303), partly to classify sherds that were less maroon in color than Wingate Black-on-red, but also to include in a classification a certain fuzziness of the edges of painted motifs, defined as a type North Plains Black-on-red. But I have been unable to find any correlation between this coloration and fuzziness, and Olson himself (1959: 134) has since cast doubt on his original classification. In addition, North Plains Black-on-red, described by Dittert (1959: 408-9), is not considered a synonym for Wingate Black-on-red because Gladwin's unillustrated short description of Wingate Black-on-red proved inadequate for so close a comparison. Nor am I sure that Dittert, Olson, and Wasley have been using North Plains Black-on-red as a type name for the same thing, for Dittert (1959: 408-9) lists North Plains Black-on-red as a type belonging to the Kowina Phase in the Acoma area, which dates from A.D. 1200 to 1400, whereas Wasley (1959: 219) lists North Plains Black-on-red as an intrusive type in Ceramic Period E at Cerro Colorado, with dates of

A.D. 1000 to 1100. This temporal span of A.D. 1000 to 1400 does not seem likely. Furthermore, the type specimens illustrated by Gladwin (1945, Pl. 40) do not come from the Wingate Phase sites on which he was reporting (this is never brought out in his text), nor are they actually more "maroon" in color than other Wingate Black-on-red specimens.

Summary Description

Wingate Black-on-red pots are slipped red on the interior and exterior of bowls, and on the exterior of jars. The paste is light colored with sherd temper. The most typical shapes are bowls with rounded bases and walls which either incurve gently at the rim or become vertical just below the rim, and pitchers with either long or medium length necks. Decoration goes to the rim and may either cover the whole interior of a bowl or leave the center undecorated. Motifs are composed of interlocked solid and hatched units in which the hatched unit is much wider than the solid one. Hatching lines are the same width as framing lines. The most common motifs are scrolls and frets which usually have barbed edges or appendages. The area of most common occurrence is the Cibola region in western New Mexico which centers at the Puerco River. The time range for Wingate Black-on-red is A.D. 1050 to 1200 with the greatest frequency of occurrence after A.D. 1100.

WINGATE POLYCHROME

History

Named by: New Description. The name was previously used by Mera (1934), and at the Second Southwestern Ceramic Seminar (1959).

Synonyms: Houck Polychrome, Querino Polychrome (Colton and Hargrave 1937: 121; Hawley

---

FIG. 7. Wingate Black-on-red bowls.
  a. GP-02989. Tusayan 16:3.
  b. GP-02830. Ft. Defiance 15:5.
  c. GP-02406. St. Johns 4:1.
  d. GP-03269. St. Johns 11:1.
  e. GP-02401. St. Johns 4:1.
  f. GP-01092. Tusayan 16:1.

  g. ASM A-20150. Point of Pines, Arizona W:10:78.
  h. GP-03270. St. Johns 11:1.
  i. GP-51603. New Mexico F:14:1.
  All are Wingate style. Diameter of g is 30.3 cm.

a   b   c   d

e   f   g   h

i   j   k   l

m   n   o

1950: 49; Martin and Willis 1940: 102; Olson and Wasley 1956: 303; Rinaldo 1959: 204); Little Colorado type (Roberts 1932: 111); Houck ware (Roberts 1932: 112); St. Johns Polychrome, in part (Kidder and Shepard 1936: 355); it seems likely that some sherds and vessels classified as Springerville Polychrome (Martin, Rinaldo, and Barter 1957: 98, 102; Danson 1957: 93) belong to this type.

Previous descriptions: See Synonyms.

Type site: Village of the Great Kivas, Zuni Reservation, New Mexico.

Basis of present description: Analysis of 26 whole or restorable vessels in the collections of the Arizona State Museum and the Southwest Archeological Center; reference to previous descriptions where specified; distribution based on Gila Pueblo survey.

Technology

Construction: Coiling followed by scraping.

Paste: The paste is light colored and ranges from light brown to orange-buff to light gray or white. Inclusions are white, red, buff, or black angular fragments of which some, if not all, are sherds; rounded quartz grains are also present. A carbon streak is sometimes present.

Wall thickness: 5 to 7 mm., usually 6 mm.

Paint: The black paint is either thin brown or black in color. It looks like an organic and mineral combination and is sunk into the slip. Colton and Hargrave (1937: 122) report copper, iron-carbon, and manganese. The white paint is presumably kaolin.

Application of paint: The manner in which the various slip colors are applied to bowl exteriors is described under Surface Finish. Where white paint outlines black motifs on bowl interiors, the white paint was applied after the black paint.

Surface finish: Bowl interiors are slipped with a thick red slip. Roberts (1932: 111) reports that occasionally a circular area in the bottom of a bowl interior was left without a slip; none in this collection, however, shows this feature. Bowl exteriors are treated in the following ways: (1) there is no overall exterior slip, but designs in red slip paint are applied directly over the smoothed white or orange-brown paste with which these designs contrast, and the vessels then polished over following the design - 5 bowls; (2) the same as (1) but in addition, the areas between portions of the red slip are covered over with white or buff slip paint, which is applied after the red, and both are polished following the design - 13 bowls; and (3) the entire exterior is slipped white or buff and designs in red slip paint are applied over this and polished following the design - 7 bowls.

The only jar in this collection is slipped red on the neck interior and on the exterior except for the bottom which is unslipped. Roberts (1932, Pl. 27 c) illustrates a jar with a light colored slip applied first, then decorated in black, then decorated in red.

Bowl interiors and jar exteriors are generally smoothed and polished, but remain uneven and bumpy in many instances. Polishing marks are visible except on weathered or worn specimens where the soft slip has worn off. A small amount of crazing is sometimes present. Small or large fire clouds are common on exteriors.

Slip color: The red slip color is Munsell 10R 5/6, 15 vessels; 10R 4/6, 3 vessels; 7.5R 5/6, 1 vessel; 2.5 YR 4/4, 1 vessel; 2.5 YR 5/6, 6 vessels. The color is either red or orange or in between. The whitish slip color is either white or cream. Specimens are illustrated in color by Roberts (1932, Pls. 27 a-c, 31 a-c), Judd (1954: 54), and Hough (1903, Pls. 36, 46, 48, 49).

FIG. 8. Wingate Black-on-red bowls, jars, and dipper.

a. AF 2659. Provenience unknown.

b. MNA 1/10. Vabre collection, provenience unknown.

c. GP-01498. St. Johns 6:1.

d. MNA 1428/A1827. Near Lupton, New Mexico.

e. GP-02157. Ft. Defiance 13:1.

f. ASM A-20194. Point of Pines, Arizona W:10:78.

g. AF 2660. Provenience unknown.

h. AF 2662. Provenience unknown, handles ground down.

i. MNA 23/255. Kayenta.

j. GP-01097. Tusayan 16:1.

k. GP-02373. St. Johns 4:1.

l. ASM 21923. Near Greer, Arizona.

m. GP-01090. Tusayan 16:1.

n. GP-51496. New Mexico F:14:1, Burial 50.

o. ASM A-15018. Point of Pines, Arizona W:10:111, Pit House 3, floor fill.

a, c, d, g, i-n are good Wingate style; *b* is closer to Dogoszhi style; *f* and *o* could have been classified as Puerco Black-on-red.

Diameter of *j* is 18.2 cm.

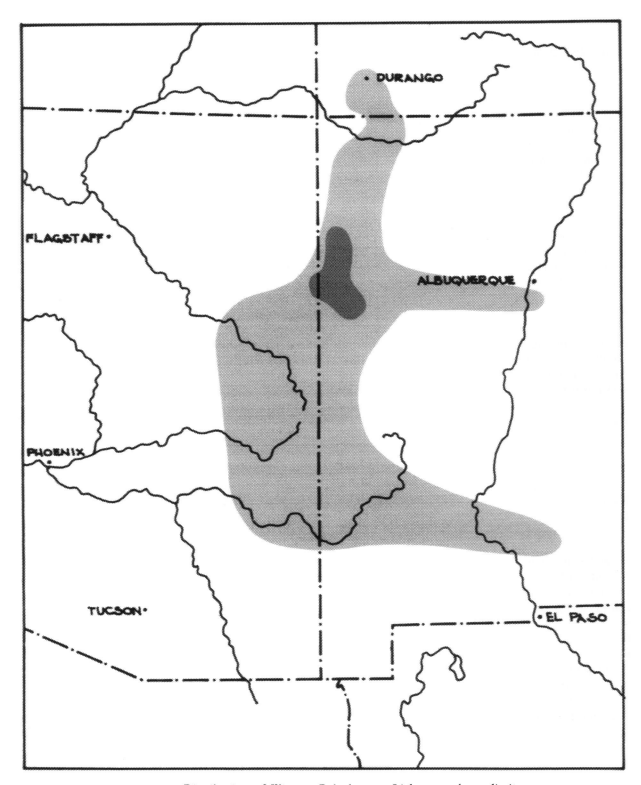

FIG. 9. Distribution of Wingate Polychrome. Light area shows limit of distribution; dark area shows greatest concentration.

Shapes

Bowls: All bowls have rounded bases. There are four shapes present on the basis of depth-diameter ratio and wall form: (1) medium depth with walls that incurve at the rim - 18 vessels; dia. 20.0 cm. - 32.7 cm.; ht. 9.1 - 15.2 cm.; incurvature 1 - 4 mm.; (2) deep with walls that incurve at the rim - 2 vessels; dia. 21.0 - 29.1 cm.; ht. 11.6 - 14.6 cm.; incurvature 2 - 7 mm.; (3) medium depth with walls that become vertical just below the rim - 4 vessels; dia. 19.2 - 26.2 cm.; ht. 9.0 - 11.4 cm.; and (4) medium depth with flaring sides - 1 vessel; dia. 20.0 cm.; ht. 8.4 cm. Bowl rims are rounded to slightly flattened self rims, 14 examples; flattened or rounded internal bevel and external lip, 4 examples; internal rounded bevel and no lip, 6 examples; flat self rim with slight internal thickening, 1 example.

Jars: The jar illustrated by Roberts (1932, Pl. 27 *c*) has a rounded body and shoulders, a short neck, and no handle. The only jar in this collection (Fig. 10 *g*) has a medium length neck, medium rounded shoulders, and a rounded body and base; dia. 14.0 cm.; ht. 13.0 cm.; it formerly had a handle which is now missing.

Dippers: Roberts (1932, Fig. 32) illustrates four dippers of this type. They are of the bowl and tubular handle form.

Painted Decoration

Fields of decoration: The fields of decoration are bowl interiors, bowl exteriors, and jar exteriors. One bowl bears rim ticking.

Color patterns: The following color patterns are found on bowls: (1) black-on-red interior with a red-and-white, cream, or buff-orange exterior, 22 examples; (2) black-and-white-on-red interior with a red-and-white (cream or buff) exterior, 2 examples; and (3) black-on-red interior with a black-on-red and white exterior, 1 example. The single vessel in this last category is the only bowl which shows a small unit design in black (Fig. 10 *b*) comparable to the "ownership marks" on Wingate Black-on-red.

Motifs on bowl exteriors: The most common motifs on bowl exteriors are an uncomplicated solid band on the walls, a white circular area on the bottom, or both. These occur on ten vessels. Other motifs which appear on one to three vessels are the following: hands, bird feet, plain or stepped frets, scrolls, stepped squares opposed by quarter terraces, and a solid white star centered on the bottom of the

bowl, or a solid cross, also on the bottom of the bowl.

Banding lines: Banding lines are narrow and are the same width as the hatching lines on 21 vessels. One bowl shows a medium width upper banding line with pendant dots; another shows an upper sawtooth edge banding line. On two bowls there is no upper banding line, and on two other bowls there is no lower banding line which leaves a negative star rather than a circle in the bowl center. Martin and Willis (1940, Pl. 102 *2*) illustrate a vessel with a double banding line in which there is a line break.

Line and motif width: Framing and hatching lines range from 1 to 2 mm., and are usually 1 mm. Uncomplicated portions of hatched motifs range from 8 to 22 mm., and are always broader than their solid segments. In this respect, the hatched motifs appear either very wide as in Wingate Black-on-red, or of medium width as in St. Johns Polychrome. Uncomplicated portions of solid motifs average 5 mm. in width. Exterior motifs are usually very wide and range from 12 to 20 mm. on intricate motifs to 50 mm. on solid bands.

Style: Twelve vessels are decorated in Wingate style, eight in Tularosa style, four in Puerco style, and two in unnamed styles.

Other Features

Rim notching: One bowl from Tusayan 16:3 exhibits four poorly-made, opposed rim notches (Fig. 11 *c*). I cannot be certain that these were intentionally made.

Spatial Distribution

The distribution is roughly the same as for Wingate Black-on-red and Puerco Black-on-red. The type occurs from slightly north of Mesa Verde, west to Holbrook, and south to just below the Gila River. One site east of the Rio Grande contained a sherd of this type. The type occurs in 83 sites in the Gila Pueblo archaeological survey of this area. The center of distribution is the Puerco River and its vicinity, as outlined in Figure 9. Thirty-three sites within this area contain the type. It is not so strongly represented either in total or in any single site as the preceding black-on-red types which suggests that it was either made in lesser quantity or occupied a shorter time span, or both. Sites containing it are more concentrated north of the core area than in any other direction which together with the center

a   b   c

d   e   f   g

h   i

indicates its close relationship to Wingate Black-on-red and Puerco Black-on-red.

Temporal Distribution

The dating of Wingate Polychrome is largely dependent on the dating of either the village of the Great Kivas (Roberts, 1932) or the Turkey Creek Ruin (Arizona W:10:78) at Point of Pines. The Village of the Great Kivas is the only well-excavated site within the core distribution area of Wingate Black-on-red, Puerco Black-on-red, and Wingate Polychrome where these three types have been found in relative abundance and where St. Johns Polychrome is either absent or of very minor occurrence. The associations at this site (Roberts 1932, Appendix) indicate that the three former types are contemporaneous, at least in part, and that they are also contemporaneous with Puerco Black-on-white, Gallup-Chaco Black-on-white, and Reserve Black-on-white. The tree-ring date of A.D. 1015 ± 15 years for this site is not a bark date and seems too early for this pottery complex. Kidder (Kidder and Shepard 1936: 355) has previously questioned this date on the basis that St. Johns Polychrome is present at the site; however, Kidder included what is defined in this study as Wingate Polychrome within St. Johns Polychrome. There is little in Roberts' description to suggest that either St. Johns Polychrome or St. Johns Black-on-red as defined here is present at the Village of the Great Kivas. The illustrated polychrome specimens are all Wingate Polychrome. Some of them exhibit a St. Johns style of decoration on the interior, but this is logical since St. Johns Polychrome appears to be a gradual lineal outgrowth of Wingate Polychrome. The complex of black-on-white pottery suggests a date of A.D. 1100 to 1200.

At the Turkey Creek Ruin at Point of Pines, Wingate Black-on-red, Puerco Black-on-red, and Wingate Polychrome all occur in relative abundance whereas St. Johns Black-on-red and St. Johns Polychrome occur in lesser amounts judging from the number of whole vessels present. These types were imported into the Point of Pines area. The material from the Turkey Creek Site has not yet been analyzed nor completely described, but the field work indicated a stratigraphic separation of St. Johns Polychrome from these other types in which it appeared later. There are unfortunately no tree-ring dates for this important site, but it has been assigned to the Reserve and Tularosa phases at Point of Pines. Pre-dating Turkey Creek at Point of Pines is Nantack Village (Arizona W:10:111) which contained both Nantack and Reserve-Tularosa Phase components and which contained small amounts of Puerco Black-on-red and Wingate Black-on-red (Breternitz 1959: 31) in what might be described as transitional Nantack-Reserve Phase associations.

At Gallo Pueblo (New Mexico F:14:1) a whole vessel of Puerco Black-on-red (Fig. 4 g), two vessels of Wingate Black-on-red (Figs. 7i, 8 n), and one vessel of Wingate Polychrome (Fig. 10 e) were found associated with Burial 50. Stylistically, the Puerco Black-on-red vessel is late, the Wingate Black-on-red vessels are typical, and the Wingate Polychrome vessel is early. The site is assigned by Barter (1957: 123) to the Reserve-Tularosa Phase with a time span of roughly A.D. 1100 to 1125.

Typological data suggest that Wingate Polychrome is an outgrowth of Wingate Black-on-red and Puerco Black-on-red, and neither of the latter can be demonstrated to have been in existence prior to A.D. 1000, or to have become common until after A.D.

FIG. 10. Early Wingate Polychrome vessels.

a. GP-02588. St. Johns 4:1.

b. GP-02365. St. Johns 4:1.

c. ASM A-17754. Point of Pines, Ariz. W:10:78, burial 25.

d. GP-01095. Tusayan 16:1. White unslipped circle on bottom.

e. GP-51608. New Mexico F:14:1, burial 50.

f. GP-02554. St. Johns 4:1. Buff unslipped circle on bottom.

g. GP-02494. St. Johns 4:1. White unslipped circle on bottom.

h. ASM A-20136. Point of Pines, Ariz. W:10:78.

i. GP-02363. St. Johns 4:1. Interior design partially restored.

a, d, e, f, h are Wingate style; *b, c, g* are Puerco style; *i* is an unnamed style.

Diameter of *d* is 26.2 cm.

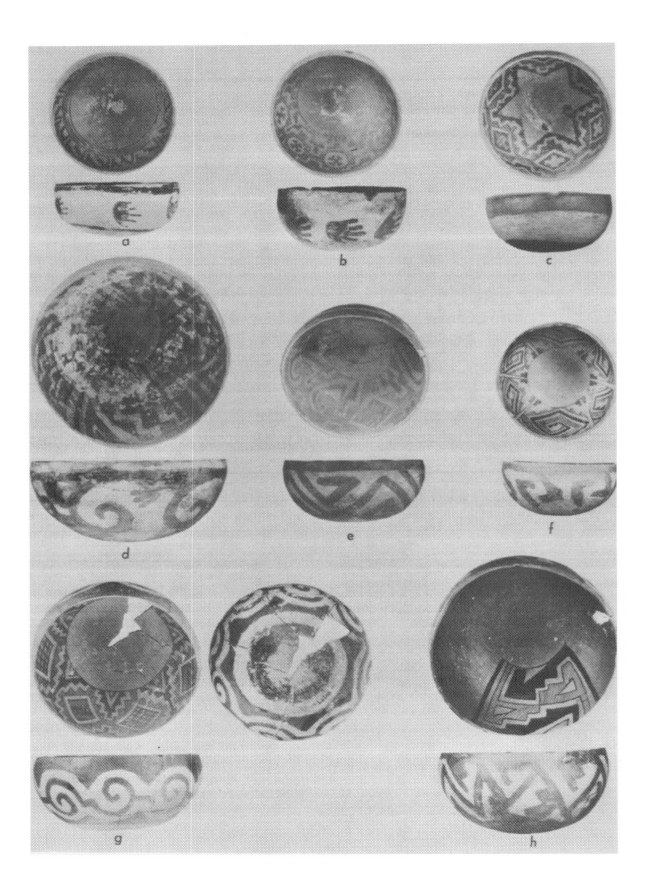

a

b

c

d

e

f

g

h

1100. I would suggest that Wingate Polychrome is most common between A.D. 1125 and 1200, but that some examples with a Tularosa style may well have been made as late as 1300.

Discussion

Some objections may be raised as to the utility of combining vessels with this amount of variation into one pottery type. The vessels could legitimately be grouped into several types on the basis of variations in one or another attribute, but it would be meaningless in the present state of our knowledge to do so, and it would be very difficult to recognize the variations in sherd form. Previous definitions for Houck and Querino polychromes, which are types that have been combined to form Wingate Polychrome, are inadequate and inconsistent. Colton and Hargrave (1937: 121-2) distinguish Houck from Querino by the absence of an exterior slip on bowls for the former type and the presence of a white exterior slip for the latter. Hawley (1950: 50) describes both as having a white exterior slip but points out that Querino has a white outlining on interiors whereas Houck does not. In this description of Wingate Polychrome all of these attributes occur as well as several others. Bowl exteriors may be unslipped with broad red design units, unslipped with broad red design units applied directly over the paste and then the remaining area covered over with white slip paint, and finally, the whole bowl exterior may be slipped white and then red designs in slip paint applied over this. Distinguishing these variations from each other when vessels are in sherd form is not easy, particularly when the unslipped paste is white and has been polished over so that it looks like a slip. However, these attributes are probably developmentally related to one another in the following sequence from early to late: (1) red designs on unslipped paste; (2) red and white designs on unslipped paste; and (3) white slip with red designs over

it. There is actually some stratigraphic evidence that red designs on unslipped paste are the earliest (Roberts 1932: 112). This whole development appears to indicate a time of experimentation with the decorative possibilities inherent in a red slip covering a white or light paste and accounts for the emergence of polychrome in this area. This development may have been stimulated, however, by polychrome tradewares whose coloration had been produced by the same method as that of Wingate Polychrome and which had come into existence earlier in the Kayenta area. The result of the experimentation was St. Johns Polychrome which bears white exterior motifs on an overall red slip.

Colton and Hargrave (1937: 121-2) grouped Houck and Querino as later than St. Johns Polychrome, possibly thinking that they formed a good developmental link between St. Johns Polychrome and the later black-and-white-on-red types such as Kwakina Polychrome and Pinnawa Polychrome. It has since been clearly shown by excavations at Point of Pines and by Olson and Wasley (1956: 304) that these types predate St. Johns Polychrome. This is also implied in Roberts' work at the Village of the Great Kivas. Rinaldo (1959: 198) is still using Querino as post-St. Johns Polychrome. Part of this problem is that some sherds which I would classify as Pinedale Polychrome exhibit interior decoration in black glaze paint and exterior decoration in red slip paint contrasted to the unslipped paste; sometimes, in addition, they bear black painted designs on the exterior. This variation in Pinedale Polychrome is rare and is known only from sherds. This "Houck" type of exterior decoration has also recently been reported on Kwakina Polychrome (Martin, Rinaldo, and Longacre 1961, Fig. 95). These few examples may either indicate a later persistence of this method of forming a polychrome into the glaze paint horizon, or a later re-emergence of this rather simple method of forming a polychrome through what Rands (1961: 331) calls

FIG. 11. Late Wingate Polychrome vessels.
- *a.* GP-01294. Tusayan 16:2.
- *b.* GP-02589. St. Johns 4:1.
- *c.* GP-02981. Tusayan 16:3.
- *d.* ASM 21974. Near Greer, Arizona.
- *e.* ASM 3905. Provenience unknown.
- *f.* GP-02555. St. Johns 4:1.
- *g.* GP-01747. Holbrook 12:1.
- *h.* GP-03022. Tusayan 16:3. Interior design partially restored.
- *a,* unnamed style; *b - h,* Tularosa style.
- Diameter of *d:* 30.5 cm.

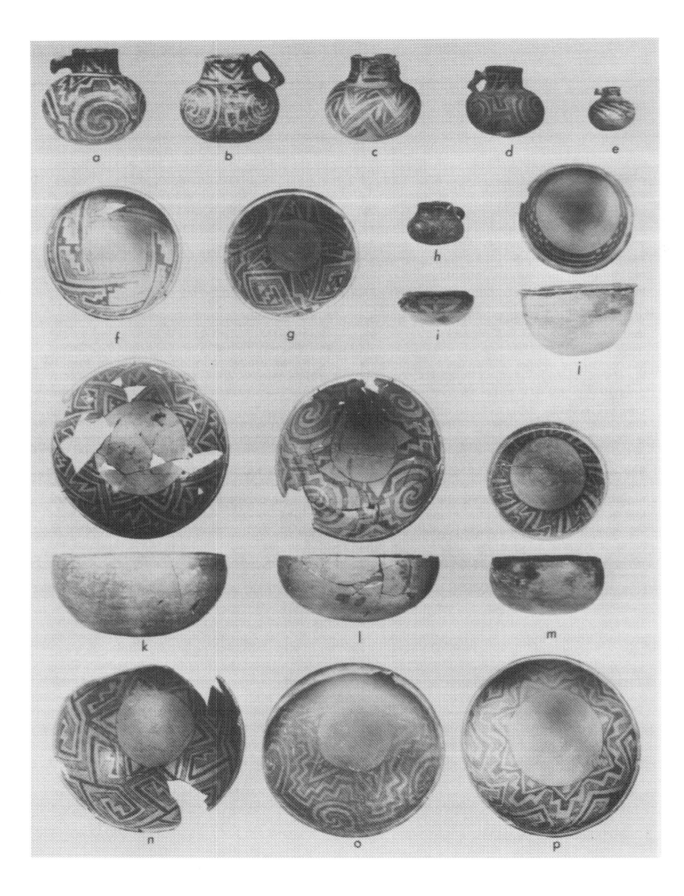

a   b   c   d   e

f   g   h   i   j

k   l   m

n   o   p

"The potter's wish to create something slightly different while remaining within the technico-stylistic bounds of a tradition." This method is not unknown on late St. Johns Polychrome bowls, for it is found on bowl interiors (Fig. 17 *h*) although never on bowl exteriors. In short, the method of forming a polychrome on bowl exteriors by contrasting red slip paint with the unslipped surface appears both early in the earliest forms of Wingate Polychrome and late in Pinedale and Kwakina polychromes, but from the present state of our knowledge, appears to be lacking in the middle period on St. Johns Polychrome. This hiatus is responsible for the highly varied time placement of types referred to as Houck and Querino polychromes.

If there were a good correlation between treatment of the exterior slip, color, and interior design I would suggest separating Wingate Polychrome into several types, but this is not possible with the available sample. As many as five types could be distinguished using various correlations on these 26 vessels. It appears more practicable to me to lump them all together, and infer that this was a time of experimentation in the development of polychrome which resulted in the standardized procedure of placing white motifs on a complete exterior red slip found on St. Johns Polychrome. I would not be surprised, however, if the Wingate Polychrome method of exterior decoration on bowls persisted to a limited degree throughout the span of St. Johns Polychrome. If such should prove to be the case, possibly an early Wingate Polychrome and a late Wingate Polychrome should be distinguished.

The name "Wingate Polychrome" was chosen because of the close distributional and stylistic relationships with Wingate Black-on-red and because of its early appearance as a type name for vessels with this decoration (Mera 1934).

Summary Description

Wingate Polychrome pots are slipped red (or orange) on the interiors of bowls and red and white on the exteriors of jars. Bowl exteriors exhibit either an overall white exterior slip bearing broad red motifs; contrasting red and white areas whereon the red was applied first, but with no overall slip of one color; or designs in red slip paint placed directly over the light paste with which they contrast. This range of exterior treatments is diagnostic for Wingate Polychrome and serves to distinguish it from St. Johns Polychrome which has an overall exterior red slip on which are placed white designs. The paste is light colored with sherd temper. Bowls are common; jars are very rare. Decoration goes to the rim and either covers the whole interior of bowls or leaves the center open. Motifs are composed of interlocked solid and hatched units, alternating solid and hatched bands or panels, or alternating solid and negative units. Hatching lines are the same width as framing lines. The most common interior motifs are interlocked solid and hatched barbed frets and scrolls, and double terraces. White outlining appears on some interior black motifs, and was applied after the black. The area of most common occurrence is the Cibola region in western New Mexico which centers around the Puerco River. The time range is A.D. 1125 to 1200 for the most part, but with a possible persistence of late forms until 1300.

FIG. 12. St. Johns Black-on-red vessels.
   a. GP-51422. New Mexico F:14:1. Glaze paint.
   b. GP-03200. St. Johns 11:1.
   c. GP-03301. St. Johns 11:1.
   d. MNA NA3290.5. Near Alma, New Mexico.
   e. MNA 1387/A2396. Near Springerville, Arizona.
   f. ASM A-19134. Point of Pines, Ariz. W:10:78.
   g. ASM 6073. Near St. Johns, Arizona.
   h. GP-01164. Tusayan 16:1.
   i. GP-03303. St. Johns 11:1. Head and tail missing.
   j. GP-03299. St. Johns 11:1.
   k. ASM A-20299. Point of Pines, Ariz. W:10:78.
   l. ASM A-20304. Point of Pines, Ariz. W:10:78.
   m. GP-19268. Near Holbrook, Arizona.
   n. ASM A-20137. Point of Pines, Ariz. W:10:78.
   o. GP-05524. St. Johns 16:1
   p. GP-01873. St. Johns 7:1.
   a - d, g, k - p are Tularosa style; *j* is Puerco style; *e, h, i* are unnamed styles; *f,* Tularosa style with some attributes of Wingate style.
   Diameter of *k*: 29.6 cm.

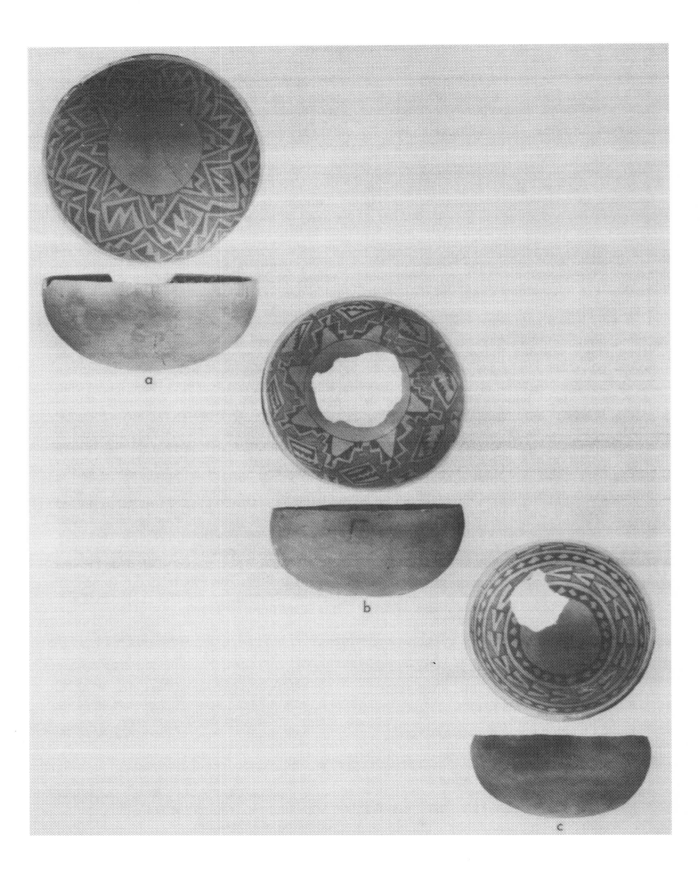

a

b

c

ST. JOHNS BLACK-ON-RED

History

Named by: Rinaldo 1959: 204-8. The name was previously used, but without detailed description.

Synonyms: Little Colorado Black-on-red, in part (Hargrave 1929: 3); Black-on-orange-red (Haury and Hargrave 1931: 104); Tularosa Black-on-red (Mera 1934: 14; Martin and Willis 1940: 165); Wingate Black-on-red, in part (Martin and Willis 1940: 165).

Previous descriptions: Rinaldo 1959: 204-8; Martin, Rinaldo, and Barter 1957: 98; Olson 1959: 118.

Basis of present description: Analysis of 35 whole or restorable vessels; reference to previous descriptions where specified.

Technology

Construction: Coiling followed by scraping.

Paste: White, gray, buff, or pink with white, red, or black angular inclusions of which the majority appear to be sherds; rounded quartz grains were noted in one vessel.

Wall thickness: 4 to 7 mm., usually 5 or 6 mm.

Paint: The black paint is probably an iron carbon mixture. In appearance it always has "fuzzy" rather than sharp edges, and is usually more brown than black. On three vessels it forms a mat glaze; on the remainder it is mat surfaced and is almost flush with the slip surface.

Surface finish: Bowl interiors and exteriors, and jar exteriors and neck interiors are slipped with a thick orange or red slip. Slipped surfaces are generally smooth and polished; marks made by the polishing tool are visible. Bowl exteriors are considerably smoother than in Wingate Black-on-red. Bumpy surfaces which were inadequately smoothed under the slip are sometimes found. The slip sometimes shows pitting over the inclusions, or the inclusions protrude through the slip. Fire clouds are present on exteriors. Some crazing is present.

Slip color: The slip color is red, orange, or in-between: Munsell 10R 5/6, 13 vessels; 10R 4/6, 6

vessels; 2.5YR 6/6, 1 vessel; 2.5YR 5/8, 2 vessels; 2.5YR 5/4, 1 vessel; 2.5YR 4/6, 1 vessel; 2.5YR 5/6, 8 vessels; 5YR 5/6, 3 vessels. One vessel is illustrated in color by Clarke (1935, Pl. 10).

Shapes

Bowls: All bowls have rounded sides and bottoms. There are three shapes: (1) medium depth with walls incurved at the rim - 14 vessels; dia. 18.7 - 30.2 cm.; ht. 9.4 - 14.4 cm.; incurvature 1 - 3.5 mm.; (2) deep with walls incurved at the rim - 5 vessels; dia. 18.7 - 30.2 cm.; ht. 10.3 - 15.4 cm.; incurvature 1 - 6 mm.; and (3) deep with sides that become vertical below the rim - 1 example; dia. 18.0 cm.; ht. 10.3 cm. Rims are internally beveled with an external lip, 14 examples; internal bevel, no lip, 1 example; and rounded self rim, 5 examples.

Jars: Two shapes are present: (1) pitchers with central rounded shoulders, rounded bodies and bases, and short or medium length necks; handles are either effigy lug handles attached just below the rim, or plain or effigy strap handles attached to the neck and body - 8 examples; dia. 13.5 - 18.5 cm.; ht. 13.0 - 18.4 cm.; (2) pitchers with quadralobate bodies and short necks - 2 examples; dia. ea. 8.6 - 17.0 cm.; ht. ca. 6.8 - 16.0 cm.; handles are strap or lug in effigy form.

Dippers: There are two dippers in the collection. Both are of the bowl and handle type. The one complete example has a total length of 29.5 cm., and a bowl width of 14.2 cm.

Eccentrics: There are three eccentrics: (1) a miniature jar with an effigy lug handle; (2) a small duck effigy vessel from which the head and tail are missing; and (3) a miniature canteen with horizontal strap handles that have been broken off and the edges ground down.

Painted Decoration

Fields of decoration: The fields of decoration are bowl interiors, jar bodies, jar necks, effigy exteriors, and handles.

Color patterns: All bowls are black-on-red on the interior, and red on the exterior. All jars are black-on-red.

FIG. 13. St. Johns Black-on-red bowls.
  a. GP-02718. Ft. Defiance 15:5.
  b. ASM 20345. Near Deming, New Mexico.
  c. GP-01872. St. Johns 7:1.

All are Tularosa style. All are the dark red color of Wingate Black-on-red.
Diameter of *a*: 30.8 cm.

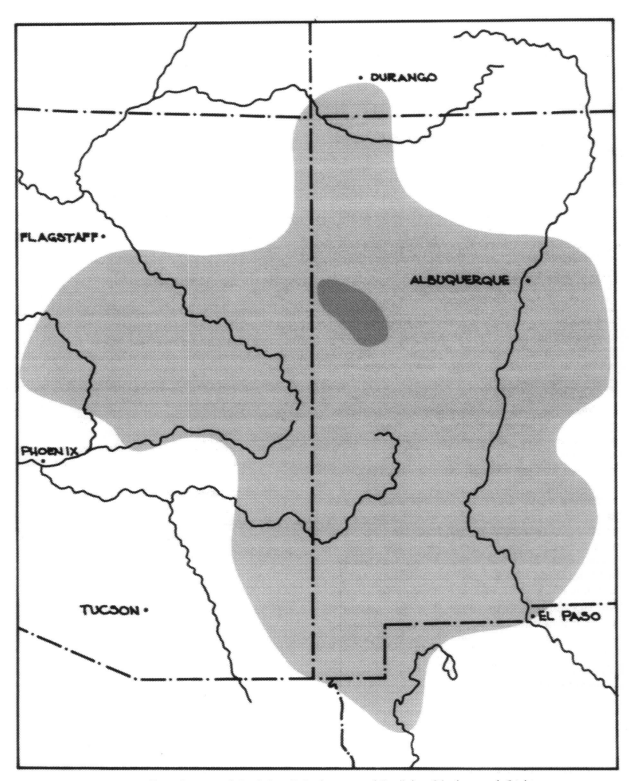

FIG. 14. Distribution of St. Johns Polychrome and St. Johns Black-on-red. Light area shows limit of distribution; dark area shows greatest concentration.

Banding lines: Banding lines are narrow and are the same width as the hatching lines. The two bowls with central figured layouts do not have banding lines.

Line and motif width: Framing lines are usually the same width as hatching lines, but in two instances are about 1 mm. wider. Framing and hatching lines range from 1 to 3 mm. in width, and are usually closest to 2 mm. Uncomplicated portions of solid linear units range from 4 to 7 mm. in width. Uncomplicated portions of hatched linear units vary from 7 to 15 mm. in width and are always wider than the corresponding solid portion of a solid and hatched motif.

Style: Twenty-eight of the 35 vessels are decorated in good Tularosa style. Two bowls are decorated in Puerco style, and one pitcher shows what is essentially Puerco style on the neck and a variant of Tularosa style, in which no solid units are present, on the body. One bowl (Fig. 12 *f*) is intermediate between Tularosa and Wingate styles. The decoration on two of the eccentrics and on one of the quadralobate jars does not conform exactly to any defined style.

Other Features

Rim notching: One pitcher, provenience unknown, shows four opposed rim notches.

Spatial Distribution

The spatial distribution is probably the same as for St. Johns Polychrome (Fig. 14).

Temporal Distribution

The temporal distribution is probably the same as for St. Johns Polychrome, A.D. 1175 - 1300. Possibly St. Johns Black-on-red has a greater frequency early in this period.

Discussion

St. Johns Black-on-red is essentially St. Johns Polychrome without white paint. It is most easily confused with Wingate Black-on-red and Pinto Black-on-red. It is most easily distinguished from Pinto on the basis of paste, slip, and surface finish. Pinto Black-on-red has a dark paste; its slip is not only thin but on bowl exteriors brown or tan areas are visible where the paste shows through; the surface is very smooth and highly polished. St. Johns Black-on-red is distinguished from Wingate Black-on-red by several attributes which occur in combination. These are an

orange or orange-red slip color as opposed to the dark red of Wingate, a much better smoothed and polished surface which is particularly evident on bowl exteriors, bowls with walls that incurve at the rim and whose rims are internally beveled with an external lip, brownish paint with fuzzy edges, and designs in which the motifs more frequently have stepped rather than barbed edges and in which the hatched units are not greatly larger than the solid ones. Certain vessels could be placed in either type. The problem here is that the attributes which cluster to distinguish one type do not change at the same rate of speed in the formation of a later type so there is bound to be overlap in both directions. The most easily recognizable of these attributes is the color shift. Wingate Black-on-red does not occur in other than red shades, whereas St. Johns Black-on-red may occur in red, orange, or orange-red.

Pitchers are much more common in St. Johns Black-on-red than in St. Johns Polychrome. The probable reason is that the area on a bowl to which white is added to form a polychrome is not present on pitchers.

All the pitchers illustrated by Martin and Willis (1940) on Plate 89, except No. 5, I would classify as St. Johns Black-on-red on the basis of design.

Summary Description

St. Johns Black-on-red vessels are slipped red, orange-red, or orange. The paste is light colored and usually has sherd temper. Bowls with walls incurved at the rim and pitchers with globular bodies are the common shapes. Decoration goes to the rim and is usually executed in interlocked solid and hatched units which frequently have stepped edges or appendages. Scrolls and frets are most common. The paint is a mat brown to black or occasionally a poor glaze. Solid motifs are used on jar necks. The type is essentially St. Johns Polychrome with no white paint added and probably occupies the same temporal and spatial distribution, although it may be more common early in this time period of A.D. 1175 to 1300.

ST. JOHNS POLYCHROME

History

Named by: Gladwin and Gladwin 1931: 36-7.
Synonyms: Black-and-white-on-red (Spier 1917: 282); three color painted ware (Spier 1919, Table 1); Little Colorado Black-on-red (Hargrave 1929: 3);

a

b

c

d

e

f

g

h

i

Chevlon ware (Hough 1930: 16); Little Colorado Polychrome (Haury and Hargrave 1931: 30); Springerville Polychrome, in part (Danson 1957: 93; Olson 1959: 12).

Previous descriptions: Haury and Hargrave 1931: 30; Colton and Hargrave 1937: 104; Kidder and Shepard 1936: 350; Hawley 1950: 49; Mera 1934: 14; Martin and Willis 1940, Pls. 97-101; Olson and Wasley 1956: 304; Martin, Rinaldo, and Barter 1957: 98; Rinaldo 1959: 201.

Type site: St. Johns 4: 1 (Gladwin and Gladwin 1931).

Basis of present description: Analysis of 100 whole or restorable vessels. Reference to previous descriptions where specified.

Technology

Construction: Coiling followed by scraping.

Paste: The paste is white to light gray, buff, pink, or occasionally black. The inclusions are black, white, red, or buff angular fragments which in most cases appear to be crushed sherds, but in some cases appear to be crushed rock or rounded quartz particles. A carbon streak is frequently present.

Wall thickness: 5 to 10 mm., usually 6 mm.

Paint: The white paint is presumably kaolin; it is soft, chalky, wears off easily, and has a tendency to absorb carbon so that it sometimes appears black. The black paint varies from a brown mat stain to a mat glaze to a shiny glaze. The latter two are less common. The mat glaze and glaze paint stand out from the slip, but where this is thin or worn away the residue looks just like that of the unglazed paint. Shepard tested the non-glazed paint from St. Johns Polychrome and noted that "the paint samples gave no test for manganese but in all cases a very much stronger test for iron than was obtained from the slip" (Kidder and Shepard 1936: 355). In the subglaze (mat glaze) variety, iron was present in all four specimens tested, copper in three, manganese in one, and faint lead in three (Kidder and Shepard 1936: 362).

Application of paint: White is used to outline black on 13 bowl interiors. On seven examples the white was applied after the black, on one example the white was applied before the black, and on five vessels I could not be certain which was applied first, but I suspect that it was the black. The one vessel (Fig. 20 c) with the white applied first is transitional in other respects to Pinedale Polychrome.

Surface finish: A thick red slip covers bowl interiors and exteriors except (1) in rare instances where the exterior bottom of the bowl is slipped white (one example, Fig. 15 h), (2) when portions of the bowl interior are left unslipped and are polished over to form part of the decoration (one example, Fig. 17 h), (3) when portions of the interior are not slipped red and are covered with white slip paint (one example, Fig. 15 b) or, (4) when the whole interior is slipped white (one example, Fig. 21 b). The last-named is transitional to Kwakina Polychrome. Of the two jars classifiable as St. Johns Polychrome, one bears a red slip on the exterior neck, shoulders, and bottom, and an unslipped buff band bearing black decoration around the exterior; the neck interior is slipped red. The other jar has an overall red slip on the exterior and neck interior. Slipped surfaces are relatively smooth and polished and narrow polishing grooves show. Bowl exteriors are much smoother than in Wingate Black-on-red and in Wingate Polychrome. On some vessels the slip has scaled off. Pitting over inclusions is common, and inclusions frequently protrude through the slip. Some crazing and small or large fire clouds are found on the exteriors of most vessels. On 12 bowls the exterior white decoration was polished over; nine of these

---

FIG. 15. St. Johns Polychrome bowls.
- *a.* GP-02414. St. Johns 4:1.
- *b.* GP-02418. St. Johns 4:1. White outlining.
- *c.* GP-6882. Showlow, Arizona
- *d.* GP-9003. San Francisco Mt. 16:3.
- *e.* ASM A-19677. Point of Pines, Ariz. W:10:78. White outlining.
- *f.* ASM 4038. Northern Arizona.
- *g.* GP-11910. Ft. Defiance 15:1.

- *h.* MNA 1511/NA789R3.22. Padre River drainage, Padre focus.
- *i.* GP-01091. Tusayan 16:1.

a, i are Puerco style; *b, c, e* are Tularosa style; *d, f, g* are Wingate style; *h* is transitional Wingate-Tularosa style.

Diameter of *c*: 30.5 cm.

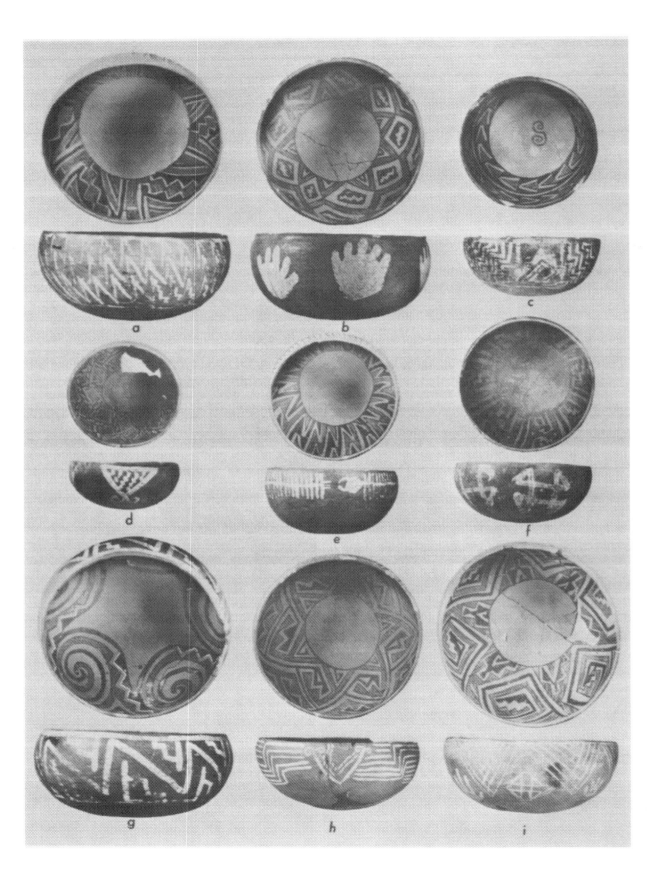

a   b   c

d   e   f

g   h   i

bowls show design characteristics similar to Wingate and Puerco styles.

Slip color: The slip color is red, orange, or in-between: Munsell 7.5R 5/6, 1 vessel; 10R 5/8, 1 vessel; 10R 5/6, 30 vessels; 10R 4/6, 6 vessels; 10R 5/4, 1 vessel; 10R 6/6, 2 vessels; 10R 6/8, 2 vessels; 2.5YR 4/8, 4 vessels; 2.5YR 5/6, 27 vessels; 2.5YR 5/4, 1 vessel; 2.5YR 4/4, 1 vessel; 2.5YR 6/6, 3 vessels; 2.5YR 5/8, 9 vessels; 2.5YR 3/6, 1 vessel; 2.5YR 4/6, 1 vessel; 2.5YR 5/4, 1 vessel; 5YR 5/6, 3 vessels; and 5YR 6/8, 2 vessels. Color illustrations have been published by Gladwin and Gladwin (1931, Pl. 35), Cummings (1940, Pl. 18), and Hough (1903, Pls. 35, 47, 63).

Shapes

Bowls: All bowls have rounded sides and bottoms. On the basis of depth-diameter ratio and wall form, there are five shapes: (1) medium depth with gently incurved rims - 76 examples; dia. 16.1 - 31.4 cm.; ht. 7.0 - 14.7 cm.; incurvature 1 - 11 mm.; (2) deep with incurved rims - 11 vessels; dia. 12.5 - 29.5 cm.; ht. 6.2 - 15.0 cm.; incurvature 1 - 10 mm.; (3) medium depth with flaring sides - 3 vessels; dia. 16.1 - 22.3 cm.; ht. 7.2 - 8.3 cm.; (4) medium depth with sides which become vertical just below the rim - 5 examples; dia. 13.8 - 22.0 cm.; ht. 6.0 - 10.7 cm.; and (5) medium depth with relatively sharp shoulders - 1 example; dia. 31.0 cm.; ht. 13.2 cm.; incurvature 7 mm. Bowl rims show an internal rounded bevel with no lip, 29 examples; internal rounded bevel and external lip, 22 examples; internal flattened bevel and external lip, 11 examples; rounded self rims with no bevel, 22 examples; a flat internal bevel, no lip, 9 examples; and internal thickening with a slight bevel and an external lip, 3 examples. Kidder and Shepard (1936, Fig. 287) illustrate profiles of rims.

Jars: Jars are rare. Only two show white paint in addition to the black and hence are classifiable in this type. One is a pitcher with a rounded body and medium length neck; it formerly had a strap handle; dia. 8.0 cm.; ht. 8.3 cm. The other is the same shape, but had no handle; dia. 13.3 cm.; ht. 12.5 cm.

Dippers: Both dippers are of the bowl and handle type. The one complete specimen is 13.8 cm. long; the width of the bowl is 8.0 cm.

Painted Decoration

Fields of decoration: The fields of decoration are bowl interiors and exteriors; jar exteriors; dipper interiors, exteriors, and handles: and, in one instance, the interior of a jar neck. Rim ticking occurs on two bowls.

Color patterns: The following color patterns are found: (1) Black-on-red interior, white-on-red exterior, 81 bowls, 1 dipper; (2) black outlined in white on a red interior and a white-on-red exterior, 13 bowls, 1 dipper; and black outlined in white exterior, and white on neck interior, 1 jar; (3) black on a part red, part white interior and a white-on-red exterior, 1 bowl; black on a part red, part white exterior, 1 jar; and (4) black on a white interior, white-on-red exterior, 1 bowl.

Motifs on bowl exteriors: The motifs on bowl exteriors were executed in white lines of medium width. The range of exterior decorations is illustrated in Figures 15 to 21. For the most part these motifs are frets, keys, meanders, opposed half terraces, and scrolls in continuous patterns, although other motifs occur. A "centipede" encircles one bowl. In unit patterns, hands or stylized hands appear on three vessels, small bird figures appear twice, concentric squares occur once, scrolls appear twice, and triangles with squiggled line filler and hooked apex occur

FIG. 16. Frequent St. Johns Polychrome motifs.
- *a.* GP-02854. St. Johns 11:1. Mat glaze paint. White outlining.
- *b.* GP-03618. St. Johns 12:1.
- *c.* GP-02985. Tusayan 16:3.
- *d.* GP-02982. Tusayan 16:3. White outlining.
- *e.* GP-02984. Tusayan 16:3.
- *f.* GP-03273. St. Johns 11:1.
- *g.* GP-02404. St. Johns 4:1. Mat glaze paint. White outlining.
- *h.* GP-02642. St. Johns 4:1.
- *i.* GP-02411. St. Johns 4:1.

a, c - i are Tularosa style; *b* is an unnamed style closely related to Tularosa.
Diameter of *g*: 30.3 cm.

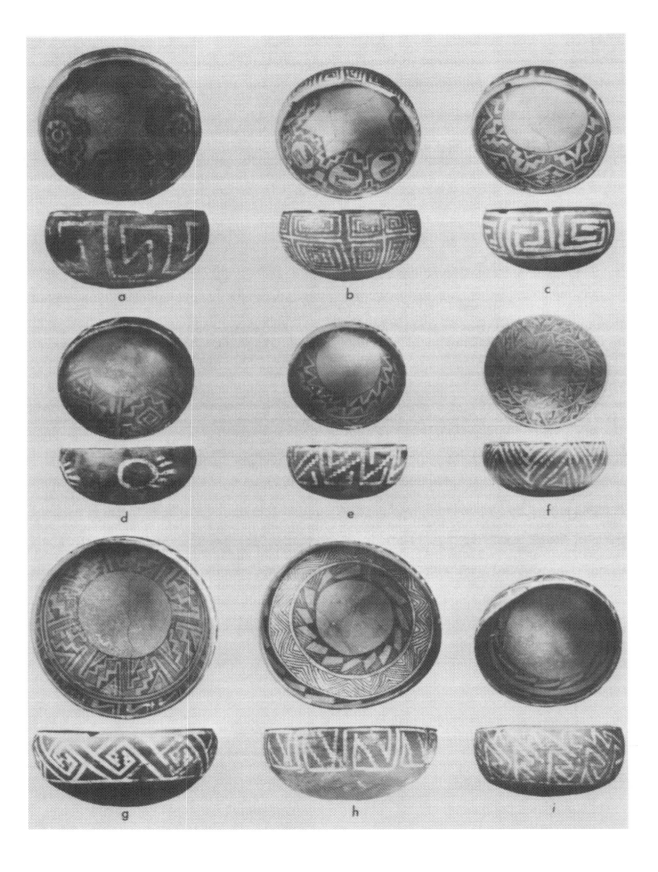

a b c

d e f

g h i

once. For the most part the motifs in unit patterns do not appear to be directly ancestral to the motifs in unit patterns on Pinedale Polychrome, nor is there much correlation between exterior unit patterns and interior motifs or patterns which are transitional to Pinedale Polychrome.

Banding lines: Banding lines are usually the same size as hatching and framing lines. In a few instances, where very fine line hatching is employed, the banding and framing lines are about 2 mm. wider. Other exceptions include one instance in which the lower banding line is 5 mm. wide, one instance in which a 5 mm. wide lower banding line with pendant dots is used, and many instances in which there are double banding lines. Double banding lines occur on nine bowl interiors. Of these one shows both upper and lower double banding lines with a line break in the lower one; seven show only double lower banding lines of which five have a line break, and two do not; on one the extra banding line is between two concentric bands and shows a line break. On nine vessels the upper banding line is missing, and on nine others the lower one is missing, so that a negative star is found in the bowl center.

Line and motif width: Framing lines and hatching lines range from 1 to 3 mm. The balancing banding line in double banding line arrangements ranges from 4 to 7 mm. Uncomplicated portions of solid linear units range from 4 to 8 mm., and are most commonly 5 mm. Uncomplicated linear portions of hatched motifs vary from 7 to 20 mm. and are most frequently 10 mm. Linear motifs on bowl exteriors range from 3 to 12 mm. in width, but are usually 6 or 7 mm.

Style: Sixty-seven of the 100 vessels are decorated in good Tularosa style. Four bowls exhibit a hatched network of diamond-shaped areas (Figs. 16 *b*; 18 *i*) which enclose solid filler motifs. This is not strictly speaking Tularosa style but is very closely related. Two vessels are in good Puerco style; eight are in

good Wingate style. One vessel (Fig. 15 *h*) is transitional between Wingate and Tularosa styles. Five vessels (Fig. 20 *b, g, h*) are closer to Pinedale style than to any other, and two (Figs. 20 *d*; 21 *c*) are more transitional between Pinedale and Tularosa styles. Nine bowls (Fig. 19) exhibit an unnamed style which, I suspect, belongs primarily to the central portion of the Little Colorado River area and is related to what might be called a Kintiel-Klagetoh style. On two vessels the design is too obliterated to determine the style.

Other Features

Rim notching: Six bowls show four opposed rim notches. One is from 10 miles northeast of Eagar, Arizona; one is from St. Johns 4: 1, one is from St. Johns 11:1, one is from Tusayan 16:3, and two have no provenience.

Spatial Distribution

St. Johns Polychrome has long been known as one of the most widespread of Southwestern pottery types. The distribution is from Mesa Verde on the north, east to the headwaters of the Pecos River, south to about Casas Grandes in Chihuahua, Mexico, and west to the Chino valley in Arizona. Within this area there are 275 sites in the Gila Pueblo survey whose surfaces yielded this type of pottery. The distribution is shown in Figure 14. The core area for St. Johns Polychrome is the approximate geographic center of the entire distribution. Sites bearing this type in quantity are most common in the Cibola area of west-central New Mexico from the continental divide west to near the Arizona-New Mexico border. Eighty-eight sites are found within this core area. Unlike the preceding types whose frequency outside of the core area is greatest to the north, the highest occurrence of St. Johns Polychrome is to the south and west of the core area. The type is relatively common along the Tularosa and San Francisco rivers

---

FIG. 17. St. Johns Polychrome bowls.

a. GP-02403. St. Johns 4:1. Glaze paint.
b. GP-01096. Tusayan 16:1.
c. GP-02853. St. Johns 11:1.
d. GP-01970. St. Johns 7:2.
e. GP-02978. Tusayan 16:3.
f. SAC UNCAT. Rockwell coll. E. Arizona.

g. GP-03274. St. Johns 11:1.
h. GP-05555. St. Johns 16:5. Unslipped interior band with black glaze paint.
i. GP-01492. St. Johns 6:1.
All are Tularosa style.
Diameter of *g*: 30.3 cm.

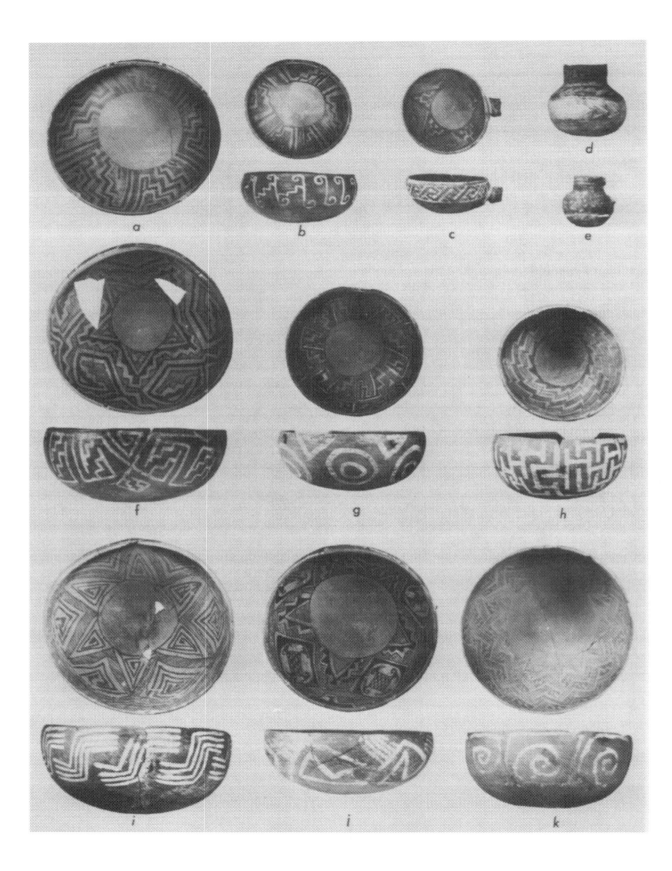

a

b

c

d

e

f

g

h

i

j

k

as far south as the Gila, and along the portion of the Little Colorado south of the junction with the Puerco River, and in the area between the Mogollon Rim and the Little Colorado. It is rare, however, between the Mogollon Rim and the Gila. I suspect that it was manufactured in the Cibola area, the Little Colorado area, and the Mogollon Rim area, but this cannot be demonstrated.

The center of the distribution is farther to the east than has been previously suggested. Gladwin (Gladwin and Gladwin 1931: 37) considered the center of distribution to be within a 50-mile radius of St. Johns, Arizona. He was probably basing this judgment on the fairly high frequency of whole vessels of St. Johns Polychrome in the Scorse collection from this area. This is an additional reason for thinking it was manufactured in this area as well as in the Cibola area, but the sherd frequencies strongly support the latter as the main center for this type. This is also reinforced by typological evidence wherein Heshota Polychrome, which centers in the Cibola area (Woodbury and Woodbury 1966), shows a stronger continuity in design from St. Johns Polychrome than does Pinedale Polychrome which centers along both edges of the Mogollon Rim.

Temporal Distribution

St. Johns Polychrome has appeared in a number of dated contexts. Haury (Haury and Hargrave 1931: 15) found it in the lower levels of the Showlow Ruin associated with tree-ring dates between A.D. 1204 and 1272, although few of these were bark dates. The type is found at Kinishba (Cummings 1940, Pl. 18) which has tree-ring dates of A.D. 1233 to 1306 (Smiley 1951: 67), but judging from the number of whole vessels, St. Johns Polychrome is extremely rare

there. It has been found as an intrusive type at LA 10 on Galisteo Creek with dates of 1241 to 1273 (Smiley, Stubbs, and Bannister 1953: 17). St. Johns Polychrome has been found in the Maverick Mountain Phase at Point of Pines along with Springerville Polychrome at Arizona W:10:50. The bark dates for this phase range from A.D. 1262 to 1293 and cluster between 1280 and 1285 (Haury 1958: 4). At Pindi Pueblo, Stubbs and Stallings (1953: 17) report St. Johns Polychrome in the fill of Kiva B with dates on small pieces of charcoal from A.D. 1213 to 1326, and in Kiva D fill with two dates at A.D. 1269. Additional dates for portions of this site with St. Johns Polychrome are given, but they encompass too long a time period to be meaningful. St. Johns Polychrome seems to date for the most part beween A.D. 1175 and 1300 and probably overlaps with Wingate Polychrome on the lower end and with Heshota Polychrome and Pinedale Polychrome on the upper end of the temporal scale.

Discussion

St. Johns Polychrome is by far the most widespread of the types in this series. It is differentiated from closely related types by the presence of white decoration over an exterior red slip on bowls. The two jars which have been included in this type description are somewhat questionable as belonging to this type, but are certainly closely related. A problem with St. Johns Polychrome is that there have been no complete reports on excavations in the late Pueblo III sites in the Cibola area which the sherd collections suggest is the most important center for this type. The preliminary report on Atsinna (Woodbury and Woodbury 1956), however, does note the high frequency of St. Johns Polychrome there. There

---

FIG. 18. St. Johns Polychrome bowls, jars, and dipper.

- *a.* GP-03277. St. Johns 11:1.
- *b.* MNA 28/273. Near Heber, Arizona. Mat glaze paint.
- *c.* GP-01064. Ft. Defiance 13:4.
- *d.* GP-02967. Tusayan 16:3. Unslipped band with black design units.
- *e.* GP-01947. St. Johns 7:2. Handle broken.
- *f.* GP-05554. St. Johns 16:15. Mat glaze paint.
- *g.* GP-03278. St. Johns 11:1. White outlining.

- *h.* GP-02366. St. Johns 4:1.
- *i.* GP-02560. St. Johns 4:1.
- *j.* ASM 16494. Turkey Hill Ruin, Flagstaff. Interior design restored.
- *k.* GP-02547. St. Johns 4:1.

a, b, d, f, g, h, j, k are Tularosa style; *c, i* are unnamed styles relating to Tularosa; *e,* design obliterated.

Diameter of *i*: 30.5 cm.

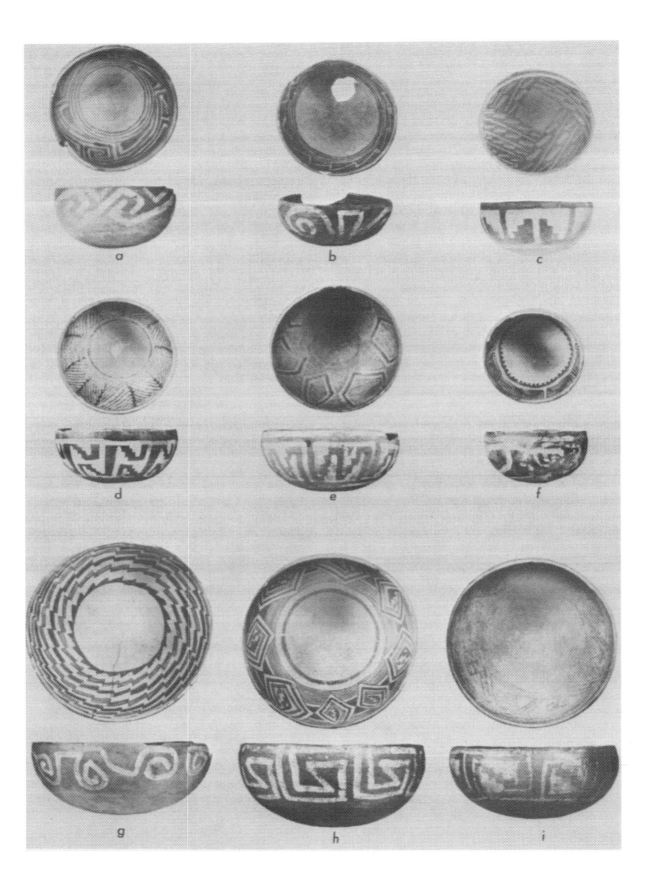

a
b
c
d
e
f
g
h
i

is no correlation between the use of white outlining on bowl interiors and other features suggestive of a transition to Pinedale Polychrome. Vessels with this attribute are best considered simply as within the range of St. Johns Polychrome. This is not unreasonable since those Pinedale Polychrome vessels which are typologically the earliest are identical to St. Johns Polychrome except in exterior decoration. Heshota Polychrome differs from St. Johns in having a thick glaze paint on interiors and narrow line white motifs on exteriors. There is a very gradual transition between these two types. The one bowl with a white interior slip appears transitional to Kwakina Polychrome. It does not bear glaze paint. The narrowness of the white line motifs on the exterior suggest that it is late.

Summary Description

St. Johns Polychrome vessels are slipped red or orange on the interior and exterior of bowls and the exterior of jars. Occasionally unslipped areas on these fields are used to form part of the decoration. The paste is light colored and usually has sherd temper. Large bowls with rounded bases and incurved rims are by far the most common forms; jars are exceedingly rare. Decoration goes to the rim and is usually executed in either interlocked solid and hatched motifs which frequently have stepped edges or appendages, or in concentric bands composed of interlocked or joined solid and hatched design units and negative fillers. Scrolls, frets, hatched double terraces with solid and negative fillers, and multiple bands are the most common motifs. Parallel hatching is most frequent, but diagonal, cross, and zigzag hatching also occur. Exterior decoration on bowls is executed in chalky white paint, and is usually in continuous patterns of linear motifs, unit patterns and some life forms, such as hands, do occur. White

may also be used on bowl interiors to outline black motifs in which cases it is usually applied after the black. The black paint is usually a dull brown or black, but is occasionally a poor glaze. The type is one of the most widespread of Southwestern pottery types and occurs throughout the Southwest. The main center of occurrence is the Cibola area, but it is reasonably common along the upper Little Colorado, in the Reserve-Tularosa area, and on the Mogollon plateau. It dates between A.D. 1175 and 1300.

SPRINGERVILLE POLYCHROME

History

Named by: Danson (1957: 93); new description.
Synonyms: Little Colorado Polychrome, in part (Haury and Hargrave 1931: 30).
Previous desriptions: Danson 1957: 93; Gifford 1957: 367; Barter 1955: 35; Martin, Rinaldo, and Barter 1957: 112; Rinaldo 1959: 204.
Type site: St. Johns 7:2.
Basis of present description: Analysis of ten whole or restorable vessels; reference to type sherds from Point of Pines; distribution based on whole vessels and sherds; quantified data refer only to whole vessels.

Technology

Construction: Coiling followed by scraping.
Paste: The paste is buff, white, or gray with or without a dark core. The inclusions are red, white, or black angular fragments of which most appear to be sherds.
Wall thickness: 5 to 7 mm., usually 6 mm.
Paint: The dark paint is either a dull brown or black and penetrates the slip, or it may be a mat glaze. The white paint is presumably kaolin; it is chalky and fugitive.

FIG. 19. St. Johns Polychrome bowls.
  a. GP-01606. Ft. Defiance 15:1.
  b. GP-01974. St. Johns 7:2. Mat glaze paint.
  c. GP-02553. St. Johns 4:1. White outlining.
  d. GP-02537. St. Johns 4:1.
  e. GP-02858. St. Johns 11:1.
  f. GP-01975. St. Johns 7:2.
  g. GP-01979. St. Johns 7:2. Mat glaze paint.

  h. GP-00916. Provenience unknown. Mat glaze paint.
  i. ASM 15615. Vandal Cave.
  a - f, h, i are in an unnamed style; *g* is Tularosa style.
  Diameter of *g*: 31.4 cm.

a   b   c

d   e   f

g   h   i

FIG. 20. St. Johns Polychrome bowls.
- *a.* GP-05553. St. Johns 16:15. Glaze paint.
- *b.* ASM 21922. Near Greer, Arizona. Glaze paint. White outlining.
- *c.* GP-02643. St. Johns 4:1. Mat glaze paint. White outlining.
- *d.* ASM A-11489. Point of Pines, Ariz. W:10:50. Mat glaze paint.
- *e.* ASM 18187. Springerville, Arizona. Glaze paint.
- *f.* GP-7882. Roosevelt 6:3, burial 5. Mat glaze paint.
- *g.* GP-8655. Arizona C:5:13, burial 3. Mat glaze paint. White outlining.
- *h.* GP-9132. San Francisco Mt. 11:2.
- *i.* ASM A-16727. Point of Pines, Ariz. W:10:50. Glaze paint.

a, c, e, f, i are Tularosa style; *b, g, h* are early Pinedale style; *d* is Tularosa-Pinedale transitional. Diameter of *g*: 31.0 cm.

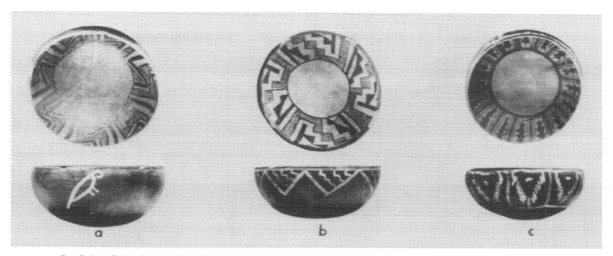

FIG. 21. St. Johns Polychrome bowls.
- *a.* SAC UNCAT. Provenience unknown. Glaze paint.
- *b.* SAC UNCAT. Provenience unknown. White slip on interior.
- *c.* SAC SB289. Coon Creek, Arizona.

a, b, Tularosa style; *c,* Tularosa-Pinedale transitional.
Diameter of *a*: 22.5 cm.

Application of paint: Both black and white are used on bowl and jar exteriors. They do not overlap in their distribution on this area and one cannot tell which was applied first.

Surface finish: A thick orange slip is applied to bowl interiors and exteriors, and to jar exteriors and neck interiors. Surfaces are smoothed, but may remain bumpy, and polished. Marks left by the polishing tool are visible. A small amount of crazing is frequently present, and fire clouds are common on exteriors.

Slip color: The slip color varies from red to reddish yellow: Munsell 2.5YR 5/6, 4 vessels; 4 YR 6/6, 3 vessels; 5YR 6/8, 2 vessels; and 10R 5/6, 1 vessel.

Shapes

Bowls: All bowls are medium depth with rounded sides and bases, and walls that incurve at the rim - nine examples: dia. 12.4 - 32.0 cm.; ht. 6.2 - 14.4 cm.; incurvature 1 - 3 mm. Rims are rounded, five examples: internally beveled and rounded, three

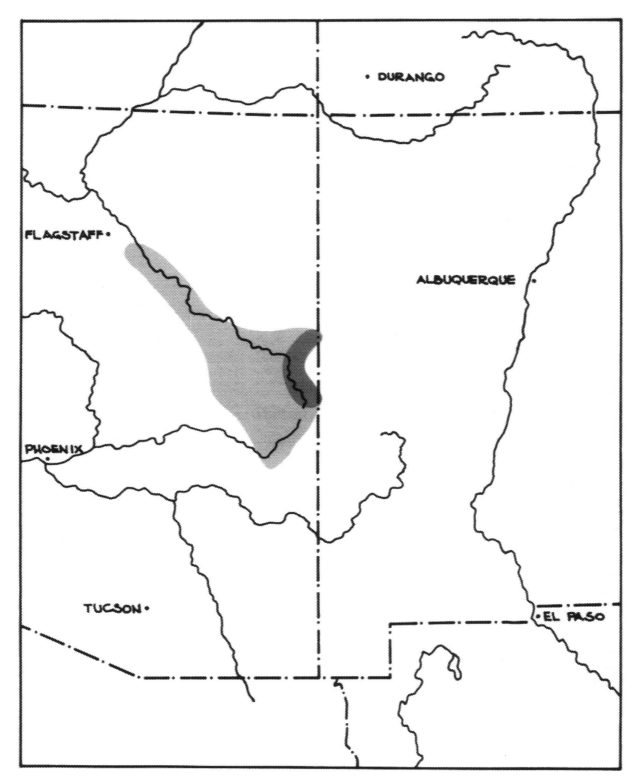

FIG. 22. Distribution of Springerville Polychrome. Light area indicates
limit of distribution; dark area shows greatest concentration.

examples: or internally beveled with an external lip, one example.

Jars: The one jar which may belong to this type has a globular body with a short neck and lug handle; dia. 13.0 cm.; ht. 11.5 cm.

Painted Decoration

Fields of decoration: The fields of decoration are bowl interiors and exteriors and jar exterior bodies and necks.

Color patterns: All bowls show black-on-red on the interior, and white-and-black-on-red on the exterior. The single jar has both black-and-white-on-red on the exterior. White predominates over black on bowl exteriors.

Motifs on bowl exteriors: Motifs on bowl exteriors are the following: solid encircling band, opposed half terraces (Fig. 23 *e*), chevrons formed of stepped squares (Fig. 23 *i*), opening running meander and encircling wavey line (Fig. 23 *a*), opposed solid triangles forming a negative zigzag (Fig. 23 *h*), and lines with flagged ends (Fig. 23 *b*).

Banding lines: Banding lines are the same width as hatching lines and range from 1 to 3 mm. wide.

Line and motif width: Framing lines and hatching lines range from 1 to 3 mm. Uncomplicated portions of solid linear motifs range from 4 to 6 mm. Uncomplicated portions of hatched linear motifs range from 7 to 12 mm. Lines on bowl exteriors range from 3 to 9 mm.

Style: Six of the vessels are in good Tularosa style. One other shows the "diamond network" motif mentioned under St. Johns Polychrome. One bowl is in an idiosyncratic style, and the last one is closest to the "Kintiel-Klagetoh" style previously mentioned under styles appearing on St. Johns Polychrome. The jar is in an unnamed style.

Spatial Distribution

Springerville Polychrome is difficult to differentiate from typical St. Johns Polychrome when small sherds are used. The sherd boards in the Gila Pueblo survey show it at only four sites. Whole vessels come from five additional sites, and on the accompanying map (Fig. 22) eight of these vessels come from sites within the area shown as the possible center of distribution. This type is known to be intrusive at Point of Pines, and the one vessel from Wupatki is probably intrusive also. Martin and Willis (1940, Pl. 98, *3*) illustrate a Springerville bowl from San

Cosmos. Haury and Hargrave (1931: 30) refer to sherds which are classifiable as Springerville Polychrome from the Showlow Ruin. It is probable that the type is also found in the Cibola area because it shows continuity into Heshota Polychrome.

Temporal Distribution

Springerville Polychrome as it has been defined here has been found in two dated contexts: (1) the lower level of the Showlow Ruin which has inconclusive tree-ring dates ranging from A.D. 1204 (Haury and Hargrave 1931: 15, 30); and (2) in the Maverick Mountain Phase at Point of Pines with dates ranging from A.D. 1262 to 1293 (Haury 1958: 4). The Maverick Mountain Phase dates are considered to date the type most reliably, and A.D. 1250 to 1300 does not seem an unlikely time range.

Discussion

Various attributes have been previously used to define Springerville Polychrome. Danson (1957: 93) used either interior white or exterior black added to typical St. Johns Polychrome as diagnostic in defining the type. Stubbs and Stallings (1953: 56) used glaze paint on otherwise typical St. Johns to define it. Rinaldo (1959: 204) used the name for sherds in which the "interior design is like Pinedale Polychrome, the exterior like St. Johns Polychrome." Barter (Martin, Rinaldo, and Barter 1957: 112) used the name for both glazed St. Johns Polychrome and for St. Johns Polychrome with white outlining the black on bowl interiors; it has thus been confused with what is classified as Wingate Polychrome. Olson (1959: 121) drops glaze paint as a diagnostic, but considers either black paint added to the exterior of typical St. Johns Polychrome vessels, or white outlining on the interior, as diagnostic. In the description proposed here, the only diagnostic is the presence of a small amount of black on the exteriors of otherwise typical St. Johns Polychrome bowls. I have yet to see a sherd or a complete vessel which uses both black on the exterior in addition to white, and white on the interior in addition to black. The latter feature occurs sporadically in Wingate Polychrome, St. Johns Polychrome, and Pinedale Polychrome but its use does not appear to be a meaningful diagnostic for differentiating these types.

The naming and the idea of a Springerville Polychrome seems to have arisen at Point of Pines in an attempt to find a transitional type between St.

a   b   c

d   e   f

g   h   i

Johns Polychrome and Pinedale Polychrome. This has not been successful. Using as the only diagnostic for Springerville Polychrome the criterion of black lines or bars added to the typically white exterior decoration of St. Johns Polychrome, makes it a late variation of St. Johns Polychrome. Thus, Springerville Polychrome and St. Johns Polychrome are developmentally precedent to Heshota Polychrome which occasionally employs the same black exterior additions to white designs on bowl exteriors. If the use of a minor amount of black on exteriors extends farther back in time than has been indicated at Point of Pines, Springerville Polychrome would lose its utility as a type. The lower level at Showlow which contains Springerville Polychrome has generally been thought to date earlier than the dating for Springerville at Point of Pines. Springerville Polychrome was originally set up as a variety of St. Johns Polychrome and it could well be classified as such. However, since it does seem to have a more restricted time range than St. Johns Polychrome; since I find it an infernal nuisance to have to specify whether Springerville is or is not included when generalizing about St. Johns Polychrome; since those people working with the type still call it Springerville Polychrome even though they may think of it as a variety; and since the type does appear to have a legitimate place in the development of Heshota Polychrome from St. Johns Polychrome, I am now calling it a type.

Summary Description

Springerville Polychrome is differentiated from typical St. Johns Polychrome by the occurrence of black lines or bars in addition to the white decoration on the exteriors of otherwise typical St. Johns Polychrome bowls. It also appears to have an orange rather than a red slip more frequently than is true for St. Johns Polychrome as a whole. It centers in the upper Little Colorado area, and appears to be diagnostic for the time period between A.D. 1250 and 1300.

PINEDALE POLYCHROME

History

Named by: Haury and Hargrave 1931: 65.

Synonyms: Red Ware (Fewkes 1904: 58); three-color glazed and painted ware (Spier 1919, Table 1); Chevlon Ware (Hough 1930: 4); Proto-Fourmile Polychrome (Haury 1930: 4).

Previous descriptions: Haury and Hargrave 1931: 67; Gladwin and Gladwin 1931: 41; Colton and Hargrave 1937: 107; Hawley 1950: 71; Rinaldo 1959: 201.

Type site: Pinedale Pueblo.

Basis of present description: Analysis of 36 whole or restorable vessels; reference to previous descriptions where specified.

Technology

Construction: Coiling followed by scraping.

Paste: The paste is usually hard and gray, but may be buff or reddish brown. Inclusions are white, red, or black angular fragments. Some of these appear to be sherds, and some of the white angular fragments look like crushed rock. A dark core is frequently present.

Wall thickness: 4 to 8 mm., usually 5 mm.

Paint: In appearance the dark paint varies from a soft organic brown stain, which has penetrated the slip, to a thick mat black or dull glaze which has not sunk into the slip. A careful inspection of vessels with the soft stain only, revealed in all cases traces of the mat black paint which suggests that it was originally there, but had worn away as a result of insufficient

---

FIG. 23. Springerville Polychrome bowls and jar.
- *a.* GP-01969. St. Johns 7:2.
- *b.* GP-01972. St. Johns 7:2.
- *c.* GP-01948. St. Johns 7:2.
- *d.* GP-01981. St. Johns 7:2.
- *e.* GP-02416. St. Johns 4:1.
- *f.* GP-02552. St. Johns 4:1.
- *g.* ASM A-16923. Point of Pines, Ariz. W:10:42.

Mat glaze paint. Drawing based on sherds.
- *h.* GP-02855. St. Johns 11:1.
- *i.* SAC W900. Wupatki Pueblo, room 25. Design restored.

a, d, e, h, i are in Tularosa style; *b, c, g,* are in an unnamed style.
Diameter of *e:* 21.3 cm.

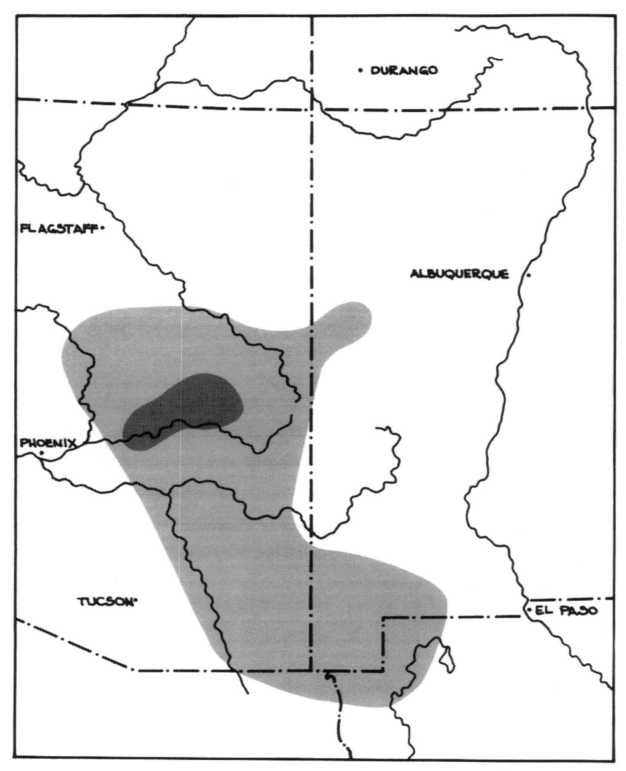

FIG. 24. Distribution of Pinedale Polychrome and Pinedale Black-on-red. Light area shows limit of distribution; dark area shows greatest concentration.

vitrification. Many vessels bearing a mat glaze or glaze show an underlying organic stain. The glaze itself is never as thick or shiny as that found on Heshota Polychrome. The minerals in the dark paint are lead, copper, and some manganese (Haury and Hargrave 1931: 65). Shepard (1942: 221) states that the copper content is very high and that lead usually occurs only as a trace, if at all. She also notes a high silica content and variability in the manganese content and silica-copper ratio. The white paint is presumably kaolin.

Application of paint: White is found on the interior or the exterior or both and was applied either before or after the black. Of the eight bowls with white on both fields, the white was applied before the black on both fields in six instances, but on two vessels it was applied on the interior before the black and on the exterior after the black. Of those bowls with white on the interior only it was applied before the black in ten instances, after the black in ten instances, and undeterminable in four instances. White is used either as a background for black design units in which case it is applied first, or as outlining for black motifs in which case it is applied either before or after the black.

Surface finish: Bowl interiors and exteriors and jar exteriors and neck interiors carry a thick red or orange slip over a well-smoothed paste. One vessel exhibits a thin watery orange slip. Narrow polishing marks are usually visible. The slip is sometimes dull and powdery, but usually has a slight sheen. Inclusions in the paste sometimes extrude through the slip. Small fire clouds are common on exteriors, and crazing is sometimes present.

Slip color: The slip color is usually red, less frequently orange: Munsell 10R 5/6, 25 vessels; 10R 5/8, 4 vessels; 10R 4/4, 1 vessel; 2.5YR 5/6, 2 vessels; 2.5YR 4/6, 1 vessel; 2.5YR 5/8, 1 vessel; 2.5YR 6/8, 1 vessel; 5 YR 7/6, 1 vessel. Color illustrations appear in Gladwin and Gladwin (1931, Pl. 38), Cummings (1940, Pls. 20, 23), and Clark (1935, Pl. 16).

Shapes

Bowls: All 33 bowls are of medium depth with rounded sides and bases and with one exception, walls that incurve at the rim; dia. 15.5 - 32.4 cm.; ht. 6.7 - 14.0 cm.; incurvature 1 - 7 mm. The one exception has walls which are vertical just below the rim. Rims are rounded self rims, 12 examples; internal rounded bevel, no lip, 15 examples; internal

bevel, slight external lip, 5 examples; and internal thickening at the rim with an internal bevel and slight external lip, 1 example.

Jars: One small pitcher with a rounded body, short neck, and effigy lug handle is present. It is very similar to St. Johns Black-on-red pitchers. A miniature jar is of the same shape, but has no handle; dia. 7.2 cm.; ht. 7.0 cm.

Dipper: One small dipper with a short handle and unperforated end is present; dia. 8.0 cm.; length 14.0 cm.

Painted Decoration

Fields of decoration: The fields of decoration are bowl and dipper interiors and exteriors, the jar neck and body as separate fields, and the dipper handle. Rim ticking is present on one small jar.

Color patterns: The following color patterns are found on bowls and the dipper: (1) black-on-red interior with a black-and-white-on-red exterior, 25 examples; (2) black-and-white-on-red interior and exterior, 8 examples; and (3) black-and-white-on-red interior and a red exterior with no design, 1 example. The jars exhibit black motifs outlined in white on a red background. On bowl exteriors the motifs may be white with details added in black, black with details added in white, black with no white, or occasionally black motifs alternate with white ones. Black motifs outlined in white are the most common.

Motifs on bowl exteriors: The following motifs are found on bowl exteriors in continuous patterns: solid black zigzag band with white dots; white zigzag band with black outlines, dots, and rattlesnake's head and tail (Fig. 26 *e*); black and white checkerboard bands (Fig. 26 *j*); black and white band of lightning (Fig. 26 *f*); white band with pendant angled lines and black edging with dots; interlocked black frets with stepped ends and white edges; black rectilinear meander with white edges; solid encircling black band edged in white (Fig. 25 *k*); solid white band at rim; black rectangles pendant from black band and edged in white (Fig. 26 *d*); and rim band with pendant diamonds edged in white (Fig. 25 *j*). All these motifs occur only once except for the checkerboard bands which occur twice. The following motifs are found in repeated unit patterns: stylized hands in black or black and white (Figs. 25 *f*; 26 *g*); black and white butterflies (Fig. 26 *h*); black diamonds with white edges and open centers (Fig. 25 *a*); black terraces with white edges and curved hook (Fig. 25 *i*);

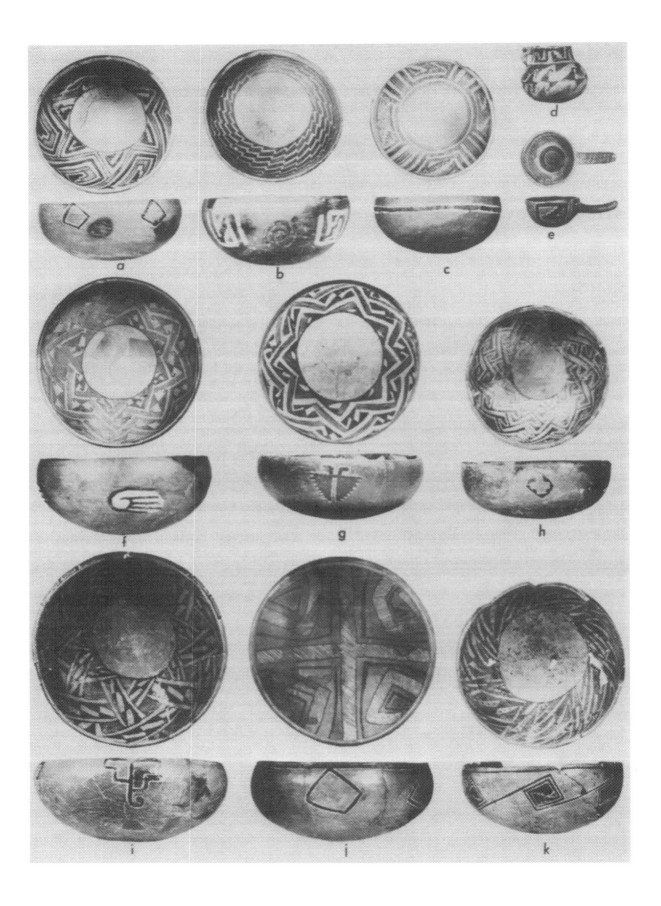

a   b   c   d

                                                              e

                    f   g   h

                    i   j   k

rectangles with negative parallelograms; rectangles with hooked lines with dotted edges (Fig. 26 *a*); frets with stepped ends (Fig. 26 *b*), terraces, and bars and stepped hooks combination. Hands and frets with stepped ends occur four times each; the others one or two times each. Motifs found in alternating unit patterns are the following: white frets alternating with black spiral or black bug (Fig. 25 *b*); quarter terraces alternating with panel with negative zigzag (Fig. 26 *i*); bird figure alternating with hourglass with fringed end (Fig. 26 *c*); and triangular frets alternating with solid horizontal bar. These combinations occur once each.

Banding lines: True banding lines are the same size as other framing lines. On five bowls there is no upper banding line present. Ten bowls show double banding lines. Five show a double lower banding line only; three show both upper and lower; and two show only a lower. None of these have line breaks.

Line and motif width: Framing lines and hatching lines are the same width and range from 1 to 3 mm., but are usually 2 mm. Balancing banding lines range from 4 to 11 mm., but are usually from 7 to 10 mm. Interior linear solid units and hatched units are usually the same width, and range from 3 to 18 mm., but are usually 10 mm. Exterior linear motifs range from 3 to 20 mm. and are usually 5 to 9 mm.

Style: Seven vessels are decorated in Tularosa style. An eighth has the "diamond network" found commonly on St. Johns Polychrome. One bowl (Fig. 25 *c*) is in Puerco style and may represent either a survival of that style or a fortuitous recombination of the same units of design. The design on the dipper could be considered as a development from Puerco style. Twenty vessels are in Pinedale style. Two bowls and two jars are decorated in an unnamed style,

closely related to Tularosa style; no hatched units are employed. Two bowls exhibit other styles.

Spatial Distribution

Pinedale Polychrome has a fairly widespread distribution (Fig. 24). It extends from the Zuni area on the northeast, westward to the Verde River and south along the San Pedro River to the Sonora border and then east into Chihuahua as far south as Casas Grandes. It is most frequent in the area of the Mogollon Rim between Roosevelt Lake and the headwaters of Silver Creek. The greatest concentrations of sherds are in sites between Roosevelt Lake and Cherry Creek. It is fairly common between the Salt and Gila rivers and much less common south of the Gila. The type itself is known to have been manufactured at the Pinedale Ruin on the headwaters of Silver Creek where sherds of unfinished vessels were recovered (Haury and Hargrave 1931: 65). Whereas the preceding types have all centered east of the Little Colorado, Pinedale Polychrome and the following types all center west of the Little Colorado.

Temporal Distribution

The most reliable dating of Pinedale Polychrome still rests on the tree-ring dates from Pinedale Pueblo where Pinedale Polychrome was associated with charcoal which gave dates between A.D. 1286 and 1330 (Haury and Hargrave 1931: 61). Smiley (1951: 68) gives 20 dates between A.D. 1280 and 1299 plus several which are markedly earlier and later for the Pinedale Ruin. At Kinishba, where Pinedale Polychrome is found, there are 75 tree-ring dates between A.D. 1233 and 1306 (Smiley 1951: 67), but the exact association of Pinedale Polychrome with the dated material is uncertain. At the Canyon Creek

---

FIG. 25. Pinedale Polychrome and Kwakina Polychrome vessels. All are Pinedale Polychrome except *g*.

   a. GP-38655. Chihuahua A:16:2.
   b. GP-02980. Tusayan 16:3.
   c. GP-10956. Roosevelt 5:8, burial 4.
   d. GP-02471. St. Johns 4:1.
   e. ASM A-9076. Near Kinishba.
   f. ASM 7109. Kinishba.
   g. ASM 3026. Kinishba. Kwakina Polychrome.
   h. ASM 23723. Kinishba.

   i. ASM 7350. Kinishba.
   j. ASM A-12724. Hilltop Ruin near Miami, Arizona.
   k. ASM A-15908. Point of Pines, Ariz. W:10:50.
a, b, f, g, i, k are Tularosa style; *c,* Puerco style; *e,* Pinedale style; *d, h,* unnamed style; *j,* idiosyncratic style.
Diameter of *i*: 32.4 cm.

a   b   c   d

e   f   g

h   i   j

Ruin tree-ring dates range from A.D. 1323 to 1348 (Smiley 1951: 72) but Pinedale Polychrome was represented by only one sherd (Haury 1934: 137). Cedar Creek Polychrome, which is in part transitional between Pinedale Polychrome and Fourmile Polychrome, also appears to be rare at this site (Morris 1957: 52) where Fourmile Polychrome was the most common decorated redware found. This suggests that both Pinedale Polychrome and its derivative, Cedar Creek Polychrome, had gone out of use prior to A.D. 1323, at least in this area.

At Point of Pines, Pinedale Polychrome is intrusive: it is found there in the Maverick Mountain and Pinedale phases dating from somewhat before A.D. 1275 to 1325 (Breternitz, Gifford, and Olson 1957: 414). These dates seem the best approximation for the duration of Pinedale Polychrome. Possibly it went out of use slightly earlier than this judging from the scarcity of it and of Cedar Creek Polychrome at the Canyon Creek Ruin, although this difference may well be a spatial rather than a temporal one.

Discussion

Typologically Pinedale Polychrome appears to be an outgrowth of St. Johns Polychrome. Its distribution centers much farther west than St. Johns Polychrome. Chronologically it is later than St. Johns Polychrome. Consequently it appears to be a lateral extension of St. Johns Polychrome through space, as well as a lineal outgrowth through time. Since St. Johns Polychrome appears in the core area of Pinedale Polychrome, it was probably made there, but in limited quantity.

As a type to be differentiated from other types in the White Mountain Redwares, Pinedale Polychrome actually represents a correlation between the use of glaze (or mat glaze) paint, the use of both black and white on any field, and the use of exterior decoration on bowls in unit patterns. The continuous patterns on some bowl exteriors remove them from this correlation, but these are, in turn, transitional to the continuous patterns in St. Johns Polychrome, on one hand, and to Cedar Creek Polychrome, on the other.

Summary Description

Pinedale Polychrome vessels are slipped red or orange on the interiors and exteriors of bowls and dippers, and on the exteriors and neck interiors of jars. The paste is light colored and usually has sherd temper. Bowls with rounded bases and incurved rims are the most common forms. Interior decoration goes to the rim and either leaves the center undecorated or covers it. Interior decoration is usually executed in interlocked solid and hatched design units in black which sometimes have white outlines. The treatment is either in closely massed units or in bold broad units. Frets and closely allied forms are common. Hatching is almost invariably parallel. Squiggled line fillers are common. Exterior motifs are either black or black and white and are usually unit, although they are sometimes continuous. White is used as a background for black motifs or elements, as trimming for black motifs, or occasionally on bowl exteriors black motifs alternate with white ones. The black paint is a glaze or a mat glaze or, in cases where this has worn away, simply a dull brown stain. The area of most frequent occurrence is just above and below the Mogollon Rim. The time of occurrence is A.D. 1275 to 1325.

PINEDALE BLACK-ON-RED

History

Named by: Colton and Hargrave 1937: 106.
Synonyms: Pinedale Polychrome, in part (Haury 1932: 422).
Previous descriptions: Colton and Hargrave 1937: 106.

FIG. 26. Pinedale Polychrome bowls.
  a. GP-3138. Arizona C:5:13.
  b. GP-8622. Roosevelt 5:5, burial 3.
  c. GP-49025. Roosevelt 6:3.
  d. GP-01748. Holbrook 12:1.
  e. GP-12224. Florence 3:11, burial 11.
  f. GP-11312. Roosevelt 5:10, burial 11.
  g. ASM 6287. Arizona.

  h. GP-11602. Roosevelt 5:11, burial 9.
  i. ASM 20005. Kinishba.
  j. GP-7430. Globe 6:1. Gila Pueblo. Design partially restored.
  a - g, i, j are Pinedale style; h, unnamed style.
  Diameter of h: 28.3 cm.

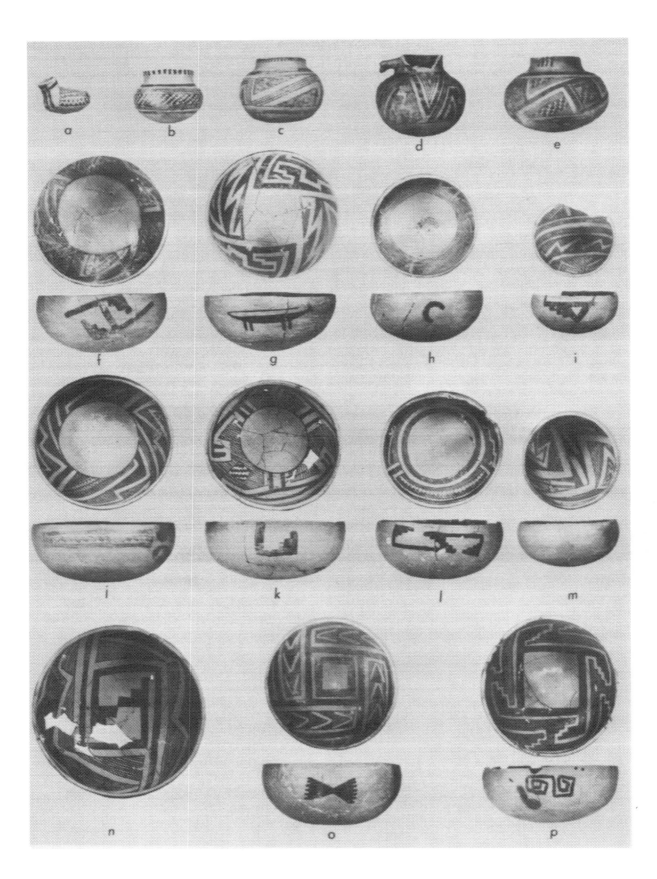

a   b   c   d   e

f   g   h   i

j   k   l   m

n   o   p

Type site: Pinedale Pueblo.

Basis of present description: Analysis of 26 whole or restorable vessels; reference to previous descriptions where specified.

Technology

Construction: Coiling followed by scraping.

Paste: The paste is usually hard and gray, but may be buff, or reddish brown. Inclusions are white, red, or black angular fragments, of which many are sherds, and some quartz sand. A dark core is frequently present.

Wall thickness: 4 to 7 mm., usually 5 mm.

Paint: The dark paint is usually a mat glaze, but grades from a dark organic stain to a shiny glaze. This gradation may occur on a single vessel. Some vessels appear to exhibit only an organic stain, but close examination shows traces of a mat glaze in all instances. The mineral constituents are probably lead, copper, and some manganese as in Pinedale Polychrome.

Surface finish: Bowls are slipped on the interior and exterior with a thick red slip. Jars are slipped on the exterior and neck interior with a red slip. One bowl is covered with a thin orange slip with specks of dark red in it. The paste is well smoothed and the slip is polished. Narrow marks left by the polishing tool are usually visible on exteriors. The slip is sometimes dull and powdery. Small exterior fire clouds are common and crazing is sometimes present.

Slip color: The slip is usually red and less frequently orange: Munsell 10R 5/6, 22 examples; 2.5YR 5/6, 4 examples. Color illustrations are given by Cummings (1940 Pl. 19).

Shapes

Bowls: All bowls are of medium depth with rounded sides and bases and incurved rims; dia. 13.6 - 24.8 cm.; ht. 6.4 - 13.6 cm.; incurvature 1 - 4 mm. Rims are internally rounded with a slight bevel, 15 examples; rounded with internal thickening at the rim, 2 examples; rounded self rims, 2 examples; and rounded with an external lip, 1 example.

Jars: Two forms of jars are present: (1) small globular jars with short vertical or slightly flaring necks and no handle - 4 examples; dia. 11.5 - 17.1 cm.; ht. 8.7 - 12.8 cm.; and (2) the same only with a single effigy lug handle and rather high rounded shoulders - 1 example; dia. 15.0 cm.; ht. 13.7 cm. I have seen sherds of larger jars than these.

Eccentrics: A single small duck effigy vessel (Fig. 27 *a*) is present in this collection. The tail, which was perforated, is missing.

Painted Decoration

Fields of decoration: The fields of decoration are bowl interiors and exteriors, jar bodies, jar necks, jar rims, and the exterior of the effigy.

Color patterns: Color patterns on bowls are black-on-red interior and exterior, 18 vessels; black-on-red interior with red exterior (no decoration), 2 vessels. The jars are all black-on-red on the exterior.

Motifs on bowl exteriors: The following motifs are found on bowl exteriors: keys; quadruped with a long tail; hourglass with fringed ends; crescents; frets with stepped ends; triangle with stepped edge; rectangles of parallel hatching with dotted edge; "S" frets; stylized hands; diamonds with a negative cross; rectangles with stepped line filler; square with barbed

---

FIG. 27. Pinedale Black-on-red vessels.

   a. ASM A-10941. Point of Pines, Ariz. W:10:50, burial 143.

   b. GP-49028. Roosevelt 6:3.

   c. GP-8219. Roosevelt 6:8.

   d. GP-03199. St. Johns 11:1.

   e. ASM 11337. Provenience unknown.

   f. GP-7804. Roosevelt 6:2.

   g. GP-41871. Roosevelt 3:3.

   h. GP-7903. Roosevelt 6:3.

   i. GP-12231. Holbrook 13:6.

   j. ASM A-6862. Point of Pines, Ariz. W:10:50,

burial 31.

   k. ASM A-16121. Point of Pines, Ariz. W:10:50, cremation 205.

   l. GP-8623. Roosevelt 5:5.

   m. GP-8243. Arizona C:5:8.

   n. ASM A-7636. Point of Pines.

   o. ASM 17159. Roosevelt Lake.

   p. ASM A-10917. Point of Pines, Ariz. W:10:50, cremation 33.

d is Tularosa style; remainder are Pinedale style. Diameter of *j*: 23.1 cm.

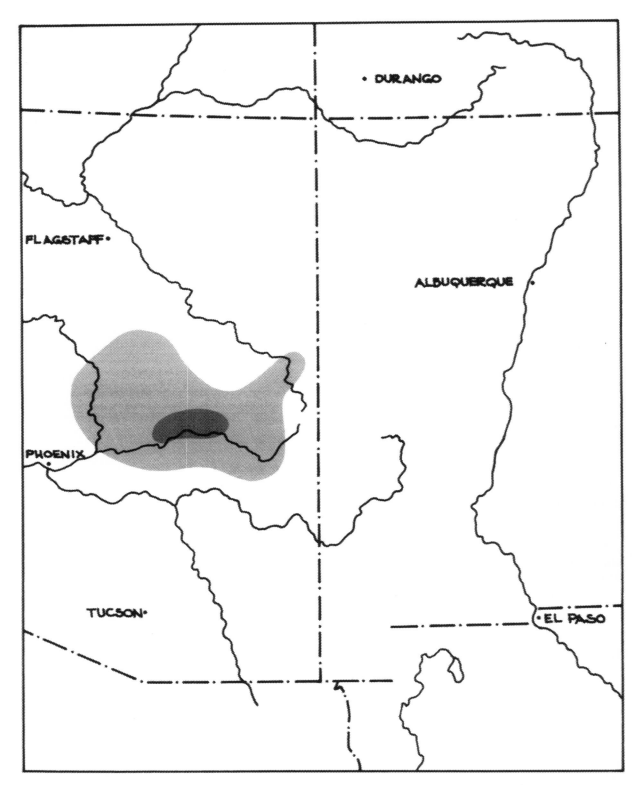

FIG. 28. Distribution of Cedar Creek Polychrome. Light area shows limit
of distribution; dark area shows greatest concentration.

edge and internal cross; and diamond with internal half terraces. All of these motifs occur in unit patterns. Frets and keys are the most common exterior motifs.

Banding lines: True banding lines are the same width as hatching lines and other framing lines. There is no painted rim band on the two bowls with negative offset quartered layouts. Four bowls show double lower banding lines and on one of these the balancing line shows two breaks which are elaborated with curved hooks on each side of the break. The others show no line breaks. One jar exhibits a double lower banding line; three show both double upper and lower banding lines. None of these contain breaks.

Line and motif width: Hatching is the same width as its framing line and ranges from 1 to 3 mm. wide, but is usually 2 mm. The hatched and solid portions of linear motifs are the same size or nearly so and range from 3 to 18 mm. in width, and are most commonly 10 mm. wide. Balancing banding lines range from 4 to 12 mm., and are usually between 7 and 10 mm. wide.

Style: Pinedale Black-on-red is decorated in both Tularosa and Pinedale styles, but only two bowls and one jar (Fig. 27 *d*) are decorated in the former.

Other Features

Rim notching: One bowl from Arizona W:10:50 at Point of Pines shows four opposed rim notches. It was the cover bowl on Cremation 33 (Fig. 27 *p*).

Spatial Distribution

Pinedale Black-on-red is very difficult to distinguish from Pinedale Polychrome in small sherds. The distribution of whole vessels of Pinedale Black-on-red follows that of Pinedale Polychrome.

Temporal Distribution

The temporal range is probably the same as for Pinedale Polychrome, A.D. 1275 to 1325.

Discussion

The value of separating black-on-red pottery from its closely associated polychrome when the only difference is a little white paint is more valuable when sorting sherds than when dealing with whole vessels. Many sherds from Pinedale Polychrome vessels are undoubtedly classified as Pinedale Black-on-red.

Summary Description

Pinedale Black-on-red vessels are slipped red or orange on the interiors and exteriors of bowls and on the exteriors and neck interiors of jars. The paste is light colored with sherd temper. Medium depth bowls with rounded sides and bases and walls incurved at the rims are the most common shapes, although jars, pitchers, and eccentrics do occur. Interior decoration on bowls goes to the rim and either leaves the center undecorated or covers it. Interior decoration is usually executed in interlocked solid and hatched design units in black. The treatment is usually in bold broad units. Barbed lines and linear units with stepped appendages are common. Hatching is almost invariably parallel and dots are frequently appended to the borders of parallel-hatched bands. Squiggled lines are common filler motifs. The black paint is a glaze or a mat glaze, or in cases where it has worn away, simply a dull brown stain. Exterior motifs on bowls are black and are arranged in unit patterns which are repeated from two to four times. They are usually rectilinear geometric forms, but sometimes life forms occur. The area of most frequent occurrence is just above and below the Mogollon Rim. The time of occurrence is A.D. 1275 to 1325.

CEDAR CREEK POLYCHROME

History

Named by: Gifford 1957: 93.
Synonyms: Transitional Polychrome (Smiley 1952: 58-66); Fourmile Polychrome, in part (Martin and Willis 1940, Pl. 105, *6-7*); Showlow Polychrome, in part (Colton and Hargrave 1937: 111); Pinedale Polychrome, in part (Martin and Willis 1940, Pl. 104, *1, 3-6*); Pinedale Fourmile Polychrome (Wheat 1952: 192).
Previous descriptions: Gifford 1957: 93.
Type site: Arizona W:10:50, Point of Pines, Arizona.
Basis of present description: Analysis of 40 whole or restorable vessels; reference to previous descriptions where specified.

Technology

Construction: Coiling followed by scraping.
Paste: Buff, white to gray, or occasionally red-brown with golden mica specks. White, black, and red

a

b

c

d

e

f

g

h

i

angular fragments appear as inclusions in the paste. Most of these are sherds; some appear to be ground rock. A dark core is frequently present.

Wall thickness: 3 to 7 mm., usually 5 mm.

Paint: The dark paint is a black or a mat glaze which sometimes has a greenish cast, particularly if applied over a white background. The white paint is presumably kaolin and is soft and chalky and wears off easily. The glaze probably has the same content as that of Pinedale Polychrome and Fourmile Polychrome.

Application of paint: White is applied after the red as a slip on jar necks, as a background, or as outlining for black design units. The white is invariably applied before the black and is used for laying out the borders of black motifs after which it remains as an outline.

Surface finish: A heavy red slip covers bowl interiors and exteriors. Jars have an overall red slip on their exteriors and neck interiors; sometimes they have an overall red slip coupled with a white slipped area on the shoulders; and sometimes the body is slipped red and the neck and shoulders and neck interior are slipped white. The red slip is smooth and well polished. Very narrow polishing marks are usually visible on interiors and exteriors, particularly on the bottoms of bowls. The white slip is thick and chalky and sometimes has a granular texture. It is not so well smoothed as the red. Fire clouds are common on exteriors.

Slip color: The color is usually red and occasionally orange: Munsell 10R 5/6, 37 vessels; 2.5YR 5/6, 3 vessels. Vessels are illustrated in color by Hough (1903, Pl. 9), Cummings (1940, Pl. 22), and Fewkes (1904, Pl. 38 *b*).

Shapes

Bowls: All bowls are of medium depth with rounded bases and sides and walls that incurve at the rim - 36 examples; dia. 15.4 - 34.2 cm.; ht. 6.0 - 15.2 cm.; incurvature 1-6 mm., usually 3 mm. Rims are of three shapes: (1) internal rounded bevel, 32 examples; (2) internal rounded bevel with rim thickening internally, 1 example; and (3) rounded self rims, 3 examples.

Jars: Jars are of three forms: (1) globular bodies with short necks which have either vertical sides or sides that are slightly concave - 2 examples; dia. 19.0 - 20.8 cm.; ht. 15.6 - 17.0 cm.; and (2) globular body with a very short flaring neck - 1 example; dia. 18.0 cm.; ht. 12.4 cm.; and (3) globular body with a very short vertical neck - 1 example; dia. 14.1 cm.; ht. 9.5 cm.; this specimen also has a suspension(?) hole on two sides at the junction of the neck and body.

Eccentrics: Hough (1903, Pl. 9) illustrates a double bowl and a small rectangular "paint cup" which appear to belong to this type. These forms are reproduced in Figure 31 *k, l*.

Painted Decoration

Fields of decoration: The fields of decoration are bowl interiors and exteriors and jar bodies, necks, and rims. Necks and rims do not always bear decoration.

Color patterns: Bowls exhibit the following color patterns: (1) white-and-black-on-red on both interior and exterior, 19 vessels; and (2) black-on-red interior and black-and-white-on-red exterior, 17 vessels. Two jars exhibit black-on-red bodies and black-on-white necks; one jar exhibits a black-and-white-on-red body and a black-on-white neck; the fourth jar has a black-and-white-on-red body, black-on-white shoulders, and a black-on-red neck interior.

Motifs on bowl exteriors: The range of exterior motifs is illustrated in Figures 29 to 31. For the most part they are either black frets or similar motifs, fine white lines, or combinations of fine white lines and black units. Black dots and white dots are sometimes used to elaborate these motifs.

Banding Lines: On 25 bowl interiors and jar exteriors the true banding lines are the same size as

---

FIG. 29. Cedar Creek Polychrome bowls.

a. GP-7545. Roosevelt 9:8.

b. GP-7828. Roosevelt 6:3, burial 1.

c. ASM A-12142. Point of Pines, Ariz. W:10:50, cremation 150.

d. GP-10683. Verde 15:30, burial 123.

e. ASM 20004. Kinishba.

f. GP-10721. Verde 15:30.

g. ASM A-18315. Point of Pines, Ariz. W:10:50, cremation 153.

h. ASM A-12198. Point of Pines, Ariz. W:10:50, cremation 153.

i. GP-7515. Roosevelt 9:5.

All are Pinedale style.

Diameter of *g*: 32.6 cm.

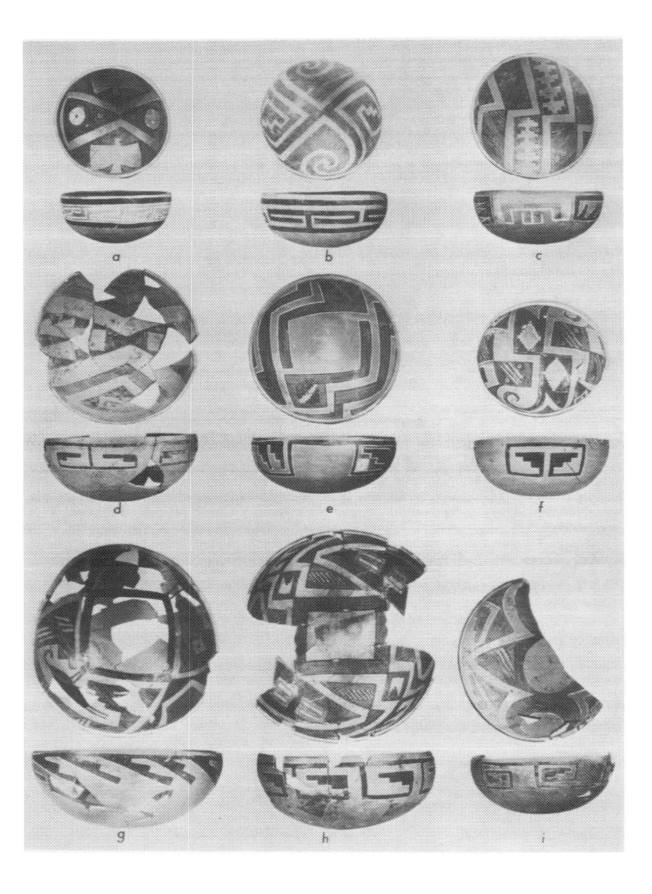

a   b   c

d   e   f

g   h   i

the hatching lines and other framing lines. On 15 bowl interiors the banding lines and other framing lines are twice the size of the hatching lines. Double banding lines occur on 13 vessels in the following combinations: (1) two jar exteriors and three bowl interiors exhibit double upper and lower banding lines; (2) one jar and one bowl show double upper banding lines only; and (3) seven bowls exhibit double lower banding lines only. None of these show breaks.

On bowl exteriors the upper banding line has a white lower border with one exception; in about half the sample it also has a white upper border. The lower banding line always has a white upper border, and in four instances also possesses a white lower border.

Line and motif width: True banding lines and framing lines on bowl interiors and jar exteriors range from 1 to 5 mm. in width and are usually 2 or 3 mm. They are either the same size as the hatching lines, which range from 1 to 3 mm., or approximately twice the size of the hatching lines. Balancing banding lines range from 7 to 11 mm. in width. Banding lines on bowl exteriors range from 4 to 11 mm. in width and are usually 6 or 7 mm. Uncomplicated portions of solid and hatched motifs are usually the same width and range from 10 to 15 mm. White lines are from 1 to 2 mm. wide.

Style: Cedar Creek Polychrome is decorated in Pinedale style. In general this style is more elaborated in Cedar Creek Polychrome than it is in Pinedale Polychrome and in Pinedale Black-on-red. Tularosa style has now completely disappeared.

Other Features

Rim notching: One jar (Fig. 31 *b*) from Cremation 80 at Arizona W:10:50 shows four opposed rim notches. It was associated with a Fourmile Polychrome bowl which was also notched.

Spatial Distribution

The distribution of Cedar Creek Polychrome is essentially the same as that for Pinedale and Fourmile polychromes, although it is not strongly represented on the sherd boards. The most northern occurrence is Homolobi from which Martin and Willis (1940, Pl. 104) illustrate a number of Cedar Creek vessels. In general it seems to center between Roosevelt Lake and the White River below the Mogollon Rim. The distribution map (Fig. 28) is based on both sherds and whole vessels.

Temporal Distribution

Cedar Creek Polychrome was first identified as a type at Point of Pines. At Arizona W:10:50/B Morris (1957: 52) states:

The early preponderance of Cedar Creek Polychrome is consistent in the sherd counts from all of the rooms in Arizona W:10:50/B, and in the light of this evidence it seems reasonable to place its predominance somewhat earlier in time than Fourmile Polychrome. Floors of increasing depth under the uppermost one, show a gradually increasing ratio of Cedar Creek Polychrome to Fourmile Polychrome, and this is the condition in the pueblo. Here the type will be provisionally dated at 1300 to 1375.

Morris also examined the type sherd collections from the Canyon Creek Ruin and the Sierra Ancha cliff dwellings and noted that these collections contain only Fourmile Polychrome and neither Cedar Creek Polychrome nor Pinedale Polychrome. However, there is one whole bowl of Cedar Creek Polychrome from Burial 30 at the Canyon Creek Ruin. The Canyon Creek Ruin itself has good tree-ring dates from A.D. 1323 to 1348 (Smiley 1951: 72). These dates plus the preponderance of Fourmile Polychrome suggest that Cedar Creek Polychrome either went out of use well toward the beginning of this

---

FIG. 30. Cedar Creek Polychrome bowls.

a. GP-11195. Globe 6:1, Gila Pueblo, burial 3.
b. GP-8208. Roosevelt 6:8, burial 2.
c. GP-11937. Verde 15:30, burial 161.
d. ASM A-6142. Point of Pines, Ariz. W:10:50.
e. ASM 21614. Kinishba.
f. ASM A-11038. Point of Pines, Ariz. W:10:50. Brown paste with golden mica and white angular inclusions.

g. ASM A-15116. Point of Pines, Ariz. W:10:50.
h. ASM 2545. Kinishba. Partially restored using composite photographs.
i. ASM A-17375. Point of Pines, Ariz. W:10:50. Brown paste with golden mica and white angular inclusions.
All are Pinedale style.
Diameter of *g*: 32.3 cm.

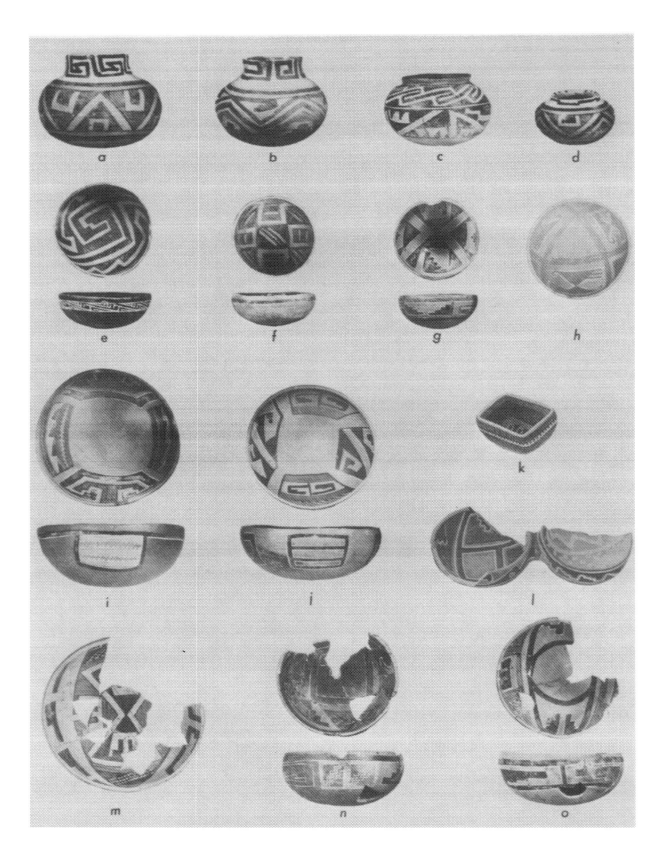

a   b   c   d

e   f   g   h

i   j   k   l

m   n   o

period or it is more common in a different area. Cedar Creek Polychrome is also found at Kinishba with tree-ring dates from between A.D. 1233 and 1306 (Smiley 1951: 67), although Cummings (1940: 20) refers to some dates as late as A.D. 1320. All these dates, however, seem somewhat too early to mark the termination of use of that site where, judging from whole vessels, Fourmile Polychrome is the predominant decorated redware. One Cedar Creek Polychrome vessel (Fig. 30 a) comes from Burial 3 in Room 75 at Gila Pueblo. This site has six dates between A.D. 1345 and 1385, but these are not considered particularly good (Smiley 1951: 61). There are also a number of vessels from the Rye Creek Ruin (Verde 15:30), but this is undated. Cedar Creek Polychrome seems to be absent or at least rare in the upper levels of the Showlow Ruin as Haury's (Haury and Hargrave 1931: 31) description of Fourmile Polychrome includes little if any of what is now called Cedar Creek Polychrome. These levels at Showlow have good dating of A.D. 1360 to 1382 (Smiley 1951: 69). Most of this evidence suggests that Cedar Creek Polychrome had disappeared by A.D. 1375 at the very latest and the suggested dates for this type are A.D. 1300 to 1375.

Discussion

Cedar Creek Polychrome has been separated from Fourmile and Pinedale Polychromes because it shows attributes which are transitional between these two types, because it is reasonably easy to identify in sherd form as well as in whole vessels, and because there is evidence that it is later in part than Pinedale Polychrome and earlier in part than Fourmile Polychrome. Several attributes distinguish it readily from

Fourmile Polychrome: the interior decoration on bowls goes to the rim, designs are always symmetrical, and framing lines are either the same size as the hatching lines or only slightly wider. The framing lines are never as heavy as in Fourmile Polychrome. This particular feature is regarded as diagnostic in distinguishing Cedar Creek Polychrome jars from those of Fourmile Polychrome. What actually appears to have happened in Fourmile Polychrome is that the heavy balancing banding lines common in Cedar Creek Polychrome become the true banding lines in Fourmile Polychrome, and that framing lines in general become broader and heavier. Cedar Creek Polychrome is distinguished from Pinedale Polychrome on the basis of exterior decoration. The use of fine white lines on bowl exteriors and the much more common use of continuous patterns in black outlined in white distinguish Cedar Creek Polychrome from Pinedale Polychrome for the most part. Both of these features of exterior decoration continue on into Fourmile Polychrome. Pinedale Polychrome rarely has fine white line decoration on the exterior of bowls. In cases where the classification of an individual vessel is questionable on any of the preceding attributes, the investigator will have to rely on other attributes. Two bowls classified as Cedar Creek Polychrome exhibit unit patterns on the exterior (Figs. 30 f, 31 j) as in Pinedale Polychrome, but the overall design treatment and the use of small white angled hooks in the decoration on one, and the use of slightly broader framing lines in the other, suggest that they belong for the most part to Cedar Creek Polychrome. There will probably not be a one-to-one correspondence in classifying transitional vessels by different investigators.

FIG. 31. Cedar Creek Polychrome bowls, jars, and eccentrics.
  a. ASM A-12313. Point of Pines, Ariz. W:10:50, cremation 185.
  b. ASM A-11249. Point of Pines, Ariz. W:10:50, cremation 80.
  c. GP-11938. Verde 16:30, burial 161.
  d. GP-9997. Roosevelt 9:20.
  e. GP-11233. Roosevelt 5:10, burial 6.
  f. ASM 17421. Roosevelt Lake.
  g. ASM A-11382. Point of Pines, Ariz. W:10:50.
  h. AF T-192. Upper Tonto Creek.
  i. GP-10567. Verde 15:30, burial 78.
  j. ASM A-16925. Point of Pines, Ariz. W:9:72.
  k. Reproduced from Hough (1903, Pl. 9). Forestdale, Arizona.
  l. Reproduced from Hough (1903, Pl. 9). Forestdale, Arizona.
  m. ASM A-15088. Point of Pines, Ariz. W:10:50.
  n. ASM A-12145. Point of Pines, Ariz. W:10:50, cremation 156.
  o. ASM A-7268. Point of Pines, Ariz. W:10:50.
All are Pinedale style.
Diameter of i: 23.2 cm.

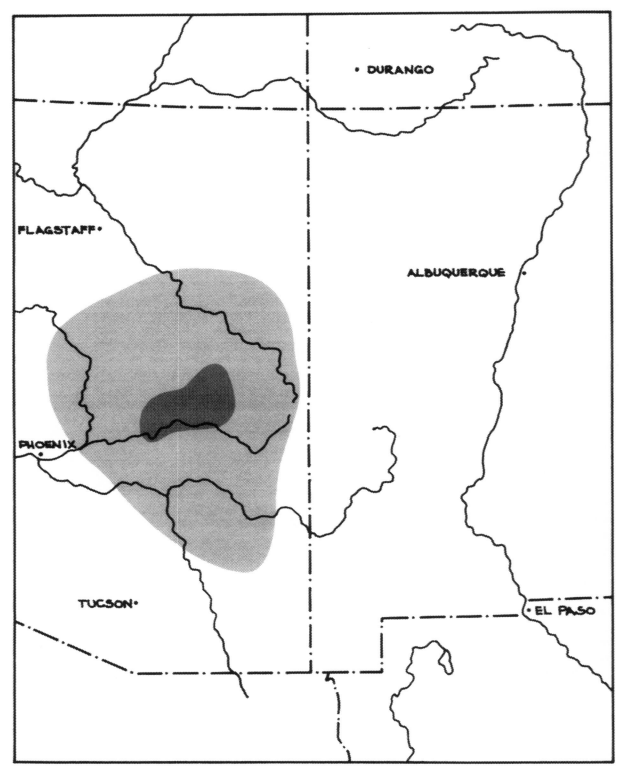

FIG. 32. Distribution of Fourmile Polychrome. Light area shows limit of distribution; dark area shows greatest concentration.

The jars classified as Cedar Creek Polychrome would formerly have been set off in a separate type, Showlow Polychrome, by virtue of having a white area on the neck and shoulders. This attribute is not diagnostic in distinguishing Cedar Creek Polychrome jars from Fourmile Polycrhrome jars, whereas the width of framing lines is. There is additional discussion of this classificatory change under Showlow Polychrome.

Summary Description

Cedar Creek Polychrome bowls are slipped red or occasionally orange on the interiors and exteriors. Jars have either an overall exterior red slip or a red slip on the body and a white slip on the neck or shoulders. The paste is usually light colored and has sherd temper. Black or mat glaze paint is used on bowl interiors and exteriors and on jar exteriors. White is used to outline some black motifs, is used as a background for design units, or forms fine line white motifs on bowl exteriors. Medium depth bowls with rounded sides and bases and incurved rims are the most common shapes, although small jars and eccentrics do occur. Interior decoration on bowls goes to the rim and is either confined to the walls or covers the entire interior. Exterior decoration usually consists of a rim band with pendant motifs outlined in white, or of a rim and base band enclosing white line motifs. However, other combinations do occur. Linear motifs consisting of interlocked solid and hatched scrolls, and broad panels, triangles, and sectors with internal solid, hatched, and negative motifs are very common on bowl interiors. Parallel hatching is usual, and rectangles with parallel hatching or with stepped line fillers are very common. Framing and banding lines are either the same size as hatching lines, or twice the size. Design treatment is bold and consists of interlocked linear units with complicated edges, large panels or sectors with internal elaboration, or combinations of the two. The area of most frequent occurrence is just above and below the Mogollon Rim. The time of occurrence is A.D. 1300 to 1375.

FOURMILE POLYCHROME

History

Named by: Haury 1930: 4.
Synonyms: Redware (Fewkes 1904: 58); Three-color glaze and painted ware (Spier 1919, Table 1);

White-bordered-black-on-red (Schmidt 1928: 294); Chevlon ware (Hough 1930: 16); Showlow Polychrome, in part (Colton and Hargrave 1937: 111); Willow Mountain Polychrome (Second Southwestern Ceramic Seminar, 1959).
Previous descriptions: Haury 1930: 4; Haury and Hargrave 1931: 31; Gladwin and Gladwin 1931: 43; Colton and Hargrave 1937: 111; Hawley 1950: 72; Martin and Willis 1940, Pls. 105-8.
Type site: Fourmile Pueblo (Holbrook 12:3).
Basis of present description: Analysis of 94 whole or restorable vessels in the collections of the Arizona State Museum, the Amerind Foundation, the Southwest Archeological Center, and the Museum of Northern Arizona; references to previous descriptions where specified; distribution based on Gila Pueblo survey.

Technology

Construction: Coiling followed by scraping.
Paste: Buff, white to gray, or occasionally red-brown with specks of golden mica. Those with red brown paste and golden mica come from Point of Pines. Inclusions are small white, red, or black angular fragments and sometimes rounded quartz grains. Most of these are sherds; some appear to be crushed rock. A dark core is usually present.
Wall thickness: 4 to 7 mm., usually 5 mm.
Paint: The dark paint, which is a glaze or mat glaze, is sometimes gritty and vitreous. It may have a greenish tinge particularly if applied over a white background. Its composition is mainly lead, copper, and some manganese (Haury and Hargrave 1931: 34). The white paint is presumably kaolin, and is soft and chalky and easily worn off. Some sherds of Fourmile Polychrome bear a purple paint in addition to black and white. No whole vessels in this collection show this treatment. Shepard (1942: 221) notes high copper and silica content, low lead content, and variable manganese in the glaze.
Application of paint: White is applied after the red either as a slip on jar necks or as a background on outlining for black design units. The white is invariably applied before the black and is used for laying out the borders of black motifs after which it then remains as an outline (Haury and Hargrave 1931, Fig. 10).
Surface finish: Bowls have a red slip on both interiors and exteriors. Jars usually have a red slipped body and a white slipped neck and upper shoulders. Some small jars have a red slip over the entire exterior

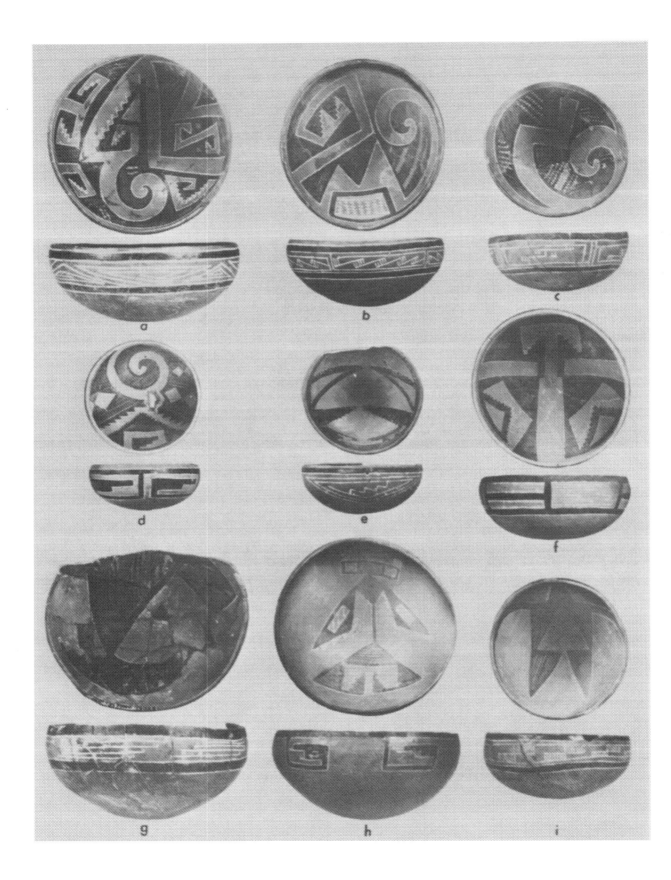

a

b

c

d

e

f

g

h

i

and a white slip on the neck interior (Martin and Willis 1940, Pls. 105-7). The paste is usually well smoothed and the slip is polished, but sometimes appears powdery. Crazing sometimes occurs: the red slip occasionally appears green in overfired specimens. The red slip is made from yellow limonite (Haury and Hargrave 1931: 32). The white slip is usually powdery and less well polished than the red, but both usually show some polishing marks.

Slip color: The slip color is usually red and occasionally orange: Munsell 10R 5/6, 77 vessels; 10R 5/8, two vessels; 2.5YR 5/6, two vessels; 2.5YR 4/6, two vessels; 2.5YR 4/8, one vessel; 10R 4/6, three vessels; undetermined, seven vessels. Vessels are illustrated in color by Hough (1903, Pl. 20); Clarke (1935, Pl. 12); Cummings (1940, Pls. 13, 17, 21, 24, 25, 32, 33); Fewkes (1904, Pls. 21-6, 29 *b*, 40, 59, 63 *b-c*).

Shapes

Bowls: Bowls occur in four shapes: (1) medium depth with rounded sides and bases, and walls that incurve at the rim, 71 vessels; dia. 13.3 - 36.8 cm.; ht. 6.3 - 18.0 cm.; incurvature 1 - 7 mm.; (2) the same as the preceding shape except that the bases taper much more toward the bottom, 3 vessels; dia. 32.0 - 37.3 cm.; ht. 15.5 - 18.0 cm.; incurvature 2 - 6 mm.; there is actually a gradation between these two shapes; (3) "flower pots," small bowls with flaring sides which join the base at a sharp angle, 3 vessels; dia. 15.7 - 18.3 cm.; ht. 7.6 - 9.0 cm.; and (4) small "squarish" bowls with straight or slightly excurvate sides which join the base at almost a right angle, 1 vessel; dia. 15.8 cm.; ht. 8.0 cm.; Martin and Willis (1940, Pl. 108, *1-3*) illustrate additional vessels of this shape. Bowl rims are direct rounded rims, 13 examples; rounded with an internal bevel, 17 examples; rounded with an internal bevel and internal thickening at the rim, 37 examples; horizontally flattened with internal

thickening, 4 examples; and undetermined, 7 examples.

Jars: Jars occur in five shapes: (1) globular body with short flaring neck, 2 examples; dia. 12.5 - 17.9 cm.; ht. 8.6 - 13.6 cm.; (2) rounded sides with walls that taper considerably toward the base, flaring neck, 1 example; dia. 19.5; ht. 13.0; (3) globular body with short straight neck, 7 vessels; dia. 14.4 - 29.5 cm.; ht. 12.9 - 23.0 cm.; (4) rounded sides with walls that taper considerably toward the base, straight necks, 3 vessels; dia. 25.2 - 35.7 cm.; ht. 18.5 - 28.5 cm.; and (5) a pitcher with a globular body, strap handle, and rather narrow vertical neck is illustrated by Fewkes (1904, Pl. 59 *b*). This is the only known example of its kind.

Eccentrics: Two complete and one fragmentary parrot effigy jars are in this collection; length 12.0 - ca. 25 cm. All possess a narrow opening in the top of the head, and rounded bodies. One has a perforated tail. Martin and Willis (1940, Pl. 105, *3-5*) illustrate Fourmile animal effigy vessels of this same general style.

Painted Decoration

Fields of decoration: All jar necks and bodies, effigy exteriors, and bowl exteriors were used as fields of decoration. One bowl has no interior decoration whatsoever, and 15 bowls have no interior decoration other than a white bordered black rim band.

Color patterns: Both black and white on a red background occur on bowl interiors and exteriors with two exceptions: one bowl has no interior decoration, not even a rim band of black outlined in white; another exhibits only black motifs on the interior. While white is used on all bowl interiors except these two, it does not outline all black motifs and on particular sherds white may not show at all. Black motifs with white outlines on a red background

---

FIG. 33. Fourmile Polychrome bowls.
- *a.* ASM 19456. Banning Wash Ruin, Cherry Creek, Arizona.
- *b.* ASM 15898. Arizona.
- *c.* GP-16450. Arizona C:2:8, Canyon Creek Ruin.
- *d.* ASM A-11392. Point of Pines, Ariz. W:10:50, cremation 84.
- *e.* GP-10748. Verde 15:30, burial 146.
- *f.* GP-16447. Arizona C:2:8, Canyon Creek Ruin, burial 30.
- *g.* GP-6994. Holbrook 12:2, Showlow Ruin.
- *h.* GP-52845. Provenience unknown.
- *i.* GP-01746. Holbrook 12:1.

All are Fourmile style.
Diameter of *g*: 37.3 cm.

a

b

c

d

e

f

g

h

i

occur on all jar bodies. Necks are either black and white or black, white, and red.

Motifs on bowl exteriors: Motifs on bowl exteriors are composed solely of fine white lines in various arrangements, of black frets, keys, barbed lines, or terraced figures, or of combinations of these black motifs with fine white lines. Small alternating black and white rectilinear birds appear on one bowl, and a black cross appears on another. Fifty-four vessels exhibit fine white lines, without black units other than banding lines. Exterior motifs are elaborated in much the same way as interior ones, but to a lesser degree. White "F" hooks are frequent, and occasionally negative stepped figures are used.

Banding lines: Banded layouts are found only on jars, on bowl exteriors, and on the "flower pot" shaped bowls. However, the remaining bowls still retain a painted banding line on the interior at the rim. All banding lines are wide. Double banding lines are absent. With the change in focus of decoration from bowl walls to bowl centers the narrow banding line appears to have gone out of use, and what was formerly the heavy balancing line becomes the true banding line. Banding lines are almost invariably black bordered in white, although a few lack the white borders altogether. The lower banding line on bowl exteriors usually has both an upper and lower white border whereas the upper banding line usually has only a lower white border. On bowl interiors the band at the rim usually has only a lower white border. Line breaks are absent.

Line and motif width: Banding lines range from 5 to 16 mm. in width, but are usually 10 mm. or very close to 10 mm. Other framing lines are usually narrower than banding lines, but are always wider than hatching lines; they range from 3 to 10 mm. in width and are usually 5 mm. If a central motif is based on the sectioning of a circle, the outer framing line is usually wider than the internal ones. Hatching

varies from 1 to 4 mm. in width, but is almost always 2 mm. White outlines are usually 2 mm. wide.

Style: Fourmile Polychrome is decorated in Fourmile style.

Other Features

Rim notching: One bowl from Cremation 80 at Arizona W:10:50 at Point of Pines shows four opposed rim notches (Fig. 35 *b*). It was associated with a Cedar Creek Polychrome jar which also has the notching.

Spatial Distribution

The spatial distribution of Fourmile Polychrome was originally worked out by Haury (1934, Fig. 23); it is in general agreement with my examination of the Gila Pueblo sherd boards. One site farther south below the Gila which contained Fourmile Polychrome was noted and the distribution was extended accordingly. Haury (1934: 130) states that

The major concentration lies east of the Sierra Ancha in an area that can be defined on the west by Cherry Creek, on the east by White River, on the south by Salt River and extending almost to the Little Colorado on the north. The focal point . . . is located below the Mogollon Rim rather than in the Silver Creek drainage.

No change in this statement seems to be indicated by present data except that possibly the core area of distribution could be shifted northward to include Homolovi where Fourmile whole vessels seem quite common (Martin and Willis 1940, Pls. 107-9). This is probably a late northward extension of the type.

Temporal Distribution

The most reliable tree-ring dates for Fourmile Polychrome come from the Canyon Creek Ruin. Cutting dates of A.D. 1326 to 1348 were obtained

---

FIG. 34. Fourmile Polychrome bowls.

a. ASM A-9084. Near Kinishba.
b. ASM 2003. Kinishba.
c. GP-850. Beaver Canyon, Verde Valley, Arizona.
d. GP-6864. Showlow.
e. AF T-195. Upper Tonto Creek.
f. GP-6862. Showlow.

g. GP-6872. Showlow.
h. ASM 7082. Kinishba.
i. ASM A-6999. Arizona W:10:50, Point of Pines.
All are Fourmile style.
Diameter of *g*: 35.4 cm.

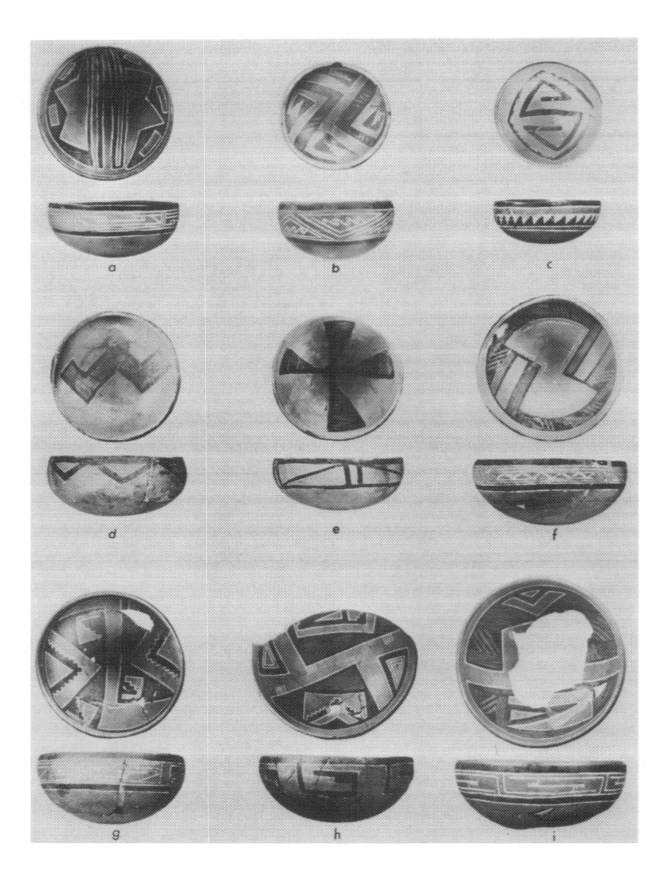

a

b

c

d

e

f

g

h

i

(Haury 1934: 55). Fourmile Polychrome was the dominant decorated pottery at the site. This suggests that Fourmile Polychrome was well developed by A.D. 1326. At the Showlow Ruin, Fourmile Polychrome was present in rooms with bark dates of A.D. 1375 to 1383 (Haury and Hargrave 1931: 41-2). At Fourmile Ruin copious amounts of both Fourmile Polychrome and Jeddito Black-on-yellow were found, but no Sikyatki Polychrome (Haury and Hargrave 1931: 42). Sikyatki Polychrome appears to have developed between A.D. 1400 and 1450 judging from the data at Awatovi (Burgh 1959: 202). At Kinishba, Fourmile Polychrome is a common decorated type. The tree-ring dates of A.D. 1233 to 1306 (Smiley 1951: 67) seem too early for dating Fourmile Polychrome. Cummings (1940: 2) estimated that the site lasted to A.D. 1350. In general, Fourmile Polychrome dates between A.D. 1325 and 1400.

Discussion

As far as the dating is concerned, Fourmile Polychrome and Cedar Creek Polychrome overlap in most of their temporal distribution. They have also been found together in cremations at Point of Pines. The data from the Canyon Creek Ruin are of interest because Cedar Creek Polychrome is virtually absent there and the tree-ring dates seem most conclusive for dating Fourmile Polychrome. This is not presently explainable on grounds of different centers of distribution for the types, but this may well be the case. The Canyon Creek Ruin is well toward the west in the area of distribution and contained abundant Fourmile Polychrome but little Cedar Creek Polychrome; Point of Pines which is well to the east in the area of distribution contained fair amounts of both types.

At Point of Pines there seems to be a regional variety of Fourmile Polychrome. Three bowls (Fig. 35 g-i) exhibit typical Fourmile style and artistry and also show local paste characteristics—brown color, presence of golden mica, and inclusions of white angular tuff.* These vessels probably date to the Canyon Creek Phase and are not only earlier than Point of Pines Polychrome, but are also much better made. It is from this variety of Fourmile Polychrome that Point of Pines Polychrome apparently originated.

Summary Description

Fourmile Polychrome bowls are slipped red or occasionally orange on the interiors and exteriors. Jars have either an overall exterior red slip or a red slip on the body and a white slip on the neck and shoulders. The paste is usually light colored and has sherd temper, but it may be light brown with rock temper. Black or mat glaze paint is used on bowl interiors and exteriors and on jar exteriors. Medium depth bowls with rounded sides and bases and walls that incurve at the rim are the most common shapes. Large and small jars, "flower pot" shaped bowls, bowls with flattened bottoms and near vertical sides, and effigies also occur. Interior decoration on bowls focuses on the center and there is usually a broad band of red background separating the interior design from the rim band. The rim band itself is a broad black band with a lower white border. Motifs on bowl interiors are large central figures, sectors spaced by background areas, or circles with either internal filler motifs or external appendages or both. Most primary motifs are black outlined in white. A large scroll with appendages is the most common motif. Large bird figures formed of various geometric units are common. Frequent filler motifs are stepped lines, dots, and solid and negative frets and stepped figures. Small white "F" hooks usually attached to stepped figures are also common. Interior patterns are either symmetrical or asymmetrical. Designs on bowl exteriors

---

FIG. 35. Fourmile Polychrome bowls.
- *a.* GP-6859. Holbrook 12:2, Showlow Ruin.
- *b.* ASM A-11250. Point of Pines, Ariz. W:10:50, cremation 80.
- *c.* ASM A-13049. Apache Reservation.
- *d.* GP-6863. Showlow.
- *e.* GP-10948. Roosevelt 5:8.
- *f.* GP-16449. Ariz. C:2:8, Canyon Creek Ruin, burial 28.
- *g.* ASM A-11046. Point of Pines, Ariz. W:10:50, cremation 42. Local paste.
- *h.* ASM A-19445. Point of Pines, Ariz. W:10:78, area B. Local paste.
- *i.* ASM A-6872. Point of Pines, Ariz. W:10:50, cremation 12. Local paste.

All are Fourmile style.
Diameter of *h*: 27.6 cm.

FIG. 36. Fourmile Polychrome bowls and jars.

a. ASM 3012. Kinishba.
b. SAC SB293. Arizona U:8:24 (?). Livingstone near mouth of Pinto Creek.
c. ASM 7135. Kinishba.
d. ASM 3009. Kinishba.
e. ASM 3024. Kinishba.
f. ASM 3052. Kinishba.

g. ASM 3043. Kinishba.
h. ASM 3037. Kinishba.
i. ASM 3011. Kinishba.
j. ASM 3051. Kinishba.
All are Fourmile style.
Diameter of h: 35.7 cm.

usually consist of series of fine white lines between two broad black banding lines just below the rim of the bowl. The banding lines are usually bordered on one or both edges in white. Rim bands with pendant black motifs, and an upper and lower black banding line enclosing black motifs are also found. Black is sometimes used as a panel divider in these bands. White "F" hooks frequently appear on bowl exteriors. Hatching is usually parallel, and framing lines are always wider than hatching lines. Jars are decorated in banded patterns containing large rectangular or triangular motifs with fillers. Jar necks exhibit either unit or continuous patterns in black. Shoulders frequently bear unit motifs. The center of abundance of Fourmile Polychrome is north of the Salt River between Cherry Creek and the White River below the Mogollon Rim. The time of occurrence is A.D. 1325 to 1400.

SHOWLOW POLYCHROME

History

Named by: Colton and Hargrave 1937: 111: new description.

Synonyms: Fourmile Polychrome, in part (Haury and Hargrave 1931: 35; 1934: 130).

Previous descriptions: See synonyms.

Type site: Showlow Pueblo.

Basis of present description: Analysis of eight whole or restorable vessels in the collection of the Arizona State Museum; reference to previous descriptions where specified.

Technology

Construction: Coiling followed by scraping.

Paste: The paste is buff, gray, or white with black, white, or red angular temper made for the most part from ground sherds. A dark core is sometimes present.

Wall thickness: 5 to 6 mm.

Paint: The black paint is a good shiny glaze. On some of the vessels it has a greenish cast, and on one poorly fired vessel it appears partly purple. The white paint is chalky and fugitive and is probably kaolin. A soft mat red-brown paint is used to contrast with the black on some vessels.

Application of paint: White is applied after the red either as a partial slip or as layout lines for black motifs. It is always applied before the black paint.

Surface finish: Bowl interiors bear either an overall white slip or a part red and part white slip. Bowl exteriors bear an overall red slip. Jars bear a white slip on the neck, shoulders, and part of the body, and a red slip on the base and part way up the sides. The surface is well smoothed, but not overly polished.

Slip color: The red slip is red: Munsell 10R 5/6. The white slip is white or slightly yellowish. Fewkes (1904, Pl. 41 *b*) illustrates a bowl interior in color.

Shapes

Bowls: Bowls occur in two shapes: (1) medium depth with rounded sides and bases and walls that incurve at the rim, 6 vessels; dia. 19.2 - 27.6 cm.; ht. 8.7 - 12.2 cm.; incurvature 1 - 2 mm.; (2) small bowls with flattened bottoms and vertical sides, one vessel; dia. 13.4 cm.; ht. 7.1 cm. Rims are internally rounded with no bevel, 2 vessels; internally rounded bevel, 3 vessels; and a rounded bevel with internal rim thickening, 2 vessels.

Jars: The one jar has a globular body with a short vertical neck; dia. 33.4 cm.; ht. 25.2 cm.

Painted Decoration

Fields of decoration: Bowl interiors and exteriors and jar sides and necks are always decorated. Rims are occasionally decorated.

Color patterns: Bowl interiors show the following color patterns: (1) black glaze and mat red brown motifs on a white background, 2 examples; (2) black glaze on a white background, 3 examples; (3) black glaze on a part white, part red background, 1 example; and (4) black glaze and mat red brown on the white portion of a red and white background, 1 example. The jar shows black glaze on a white background. Black was used for all banding lines and all primary motifs except white lines on bowl exteriors. White was used as an outline or background for black. The red-brown is used to contrast with the black-on-white backgrounds.

Motifs on bowl exteriors: Motifs on bowl exteriors consist of either motifs composed solely of fine white lines, a line with alternate white blocks, or a black diagonal line on white stepped squares with "F" hooks.

Hatching: Four vessels show no hatching, one shows only crosshatching, and three show parallel hatching.

Banding lines: Rim bands occur on all bowl interiors except one. The jar and all bowl exteriors

a

b

c

d

e

f

g

h

i

j

k

l

m

n

o

possess both upper and lower banding lines. Banding lines are either black on a white background, or black bordered in white on one or both edges. Banding lines are usually heavier than hatching lines. One rim band has pendant triangles with "F" hooks. The lower band on the jar neck has a dotted lower edge. No line breaks are present.

Line and motif width: Banding lines range from 5 to 12 mm. Other framing lines range from 4 to 6 mm. Uncomplicated portions of linear motifs range from 3 to 8 mm. and are most frequently 5 mm. Hatching lines are 2 to 3 mm. wide as are the white lines used as borders or as bowl exterior motifs.

Style: Two closely related styles of decoration appear on Showlow Polychrome. One of these can be roughly described as an arrangement of medium width linear units with flagged ends which are placed in the centers of bowl interiors. Those vessels in Figure 39 *b, e, f* illustrate this type of treatment which is for the most part absent in Fourmile Polychrome, but which is common in Kinishba Polychrome. The exteriors of these same bowls exhibit typical Fourmile Polychrome decoration. The second style employs broader, less massed units and is illustrated by Figure 39 *a, c, g*. While it resembles "Kinishba style" in some respects it is more similar to the style found on Showlow Glaze-on-white (Pseudo-Black-on-white). The interior layouts are like those found in Pinedale style in that the whole interior of bowls rather than just the center is used as a field. Exterior decoration on bowls is the same as in Fourmile Polychrome and Cedar Creek Polychrome. Showlow Polychrome appears to be transitional in style from Cedar Creek and Fourmile polychromes to Kinishba Polychrome and Showlow Glaze-on-white.

Spatial Distribution

Showlow Polychrome occupies essentially the same distribution as Fourmile Polychrome, but it is never abundant at any one site. It is found at 24 sites in the Gila Pueblo survey of this area. Martin and Willis (1940, Pl. 109, 2) illustrate one vessel from Homolovi which extends the distribution northward. While it is never very common in sites, the highest frequency of sites that contain it are below the Mogollon Rim between Cherry Creek and the White River, and this area, therefore, is indicated as the core area of distribution on the accompanying map (Fig. 38). Eleven of the 24 sites lie within this area.

Temporal Distribution

The temporal distribution appears to be the same as for Fourmile Polychrome. It is found at the Canyon Creek Ruin with dates of A.D. 1326 to 1348 (Haury 1934), at Kinishba, in the upper level of the Showlow Ruin with dates of A.D. 1375 to 1383 (Haury and Hargrave 1931: 41-2), and in the Point of Pines Phase at Point of Pines for which the suggested dating is A.D. 1400 to 1450. The Point of Pines Phase specimen may be intrusive from earlier trash. In general, Showlow Polychrome seems to date between A.D. 1325 and 1400.

Discussion

Showlow Polychrome was originally segmented from Fourmile Polychrome by Colton and Hargrave (1937: 85,111) who pointed out the use of "white paint as a *background* for a black painted decoration." What this segmentation did was to remove the

---

FIG. 37. Fourmile Polychrome bowls and jars.

a. ASM 7319. Kinishba.
b. GP-6856. Showlow.
c. ASM A-18519. Point of Pines, Ariz. W:10:50. Local paste.
d. Reproduced from Fewkes (1904, Pl. 59 *b*).
e. GP-6837. Showlow.
f. GP-6850. Showlow.
g. GP-6852. Showlow.
h. ASM A-8707. Point of Pines, Ariz. W:10:50.
i. GP-6848. Showlow.

j. GP-41877. Roosevelt 3:3, burial 3.
k. GP-16460. Arizona C:2:8, Canyon Creek Ruin, burial 37.
l. AF T-191. Upper Tonto Creek.
m. GP 6846. Showlow.
n. ASM 6293. Fourmile Ruin.
o. ASM 6294. Fourmile Ruin.
All are Fourmile style.
Diameter of *m*: 34.0 cm.

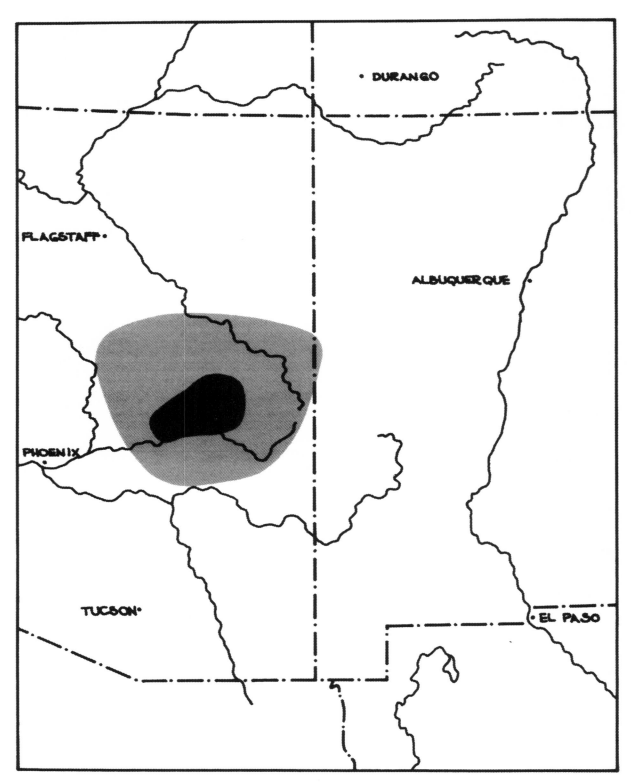

FIG. 38. Distribution of Showlow Polychrome. Light area shows limit of distribution; dark area shows greatest concentration.

Fourmile Polychrome jars from the Fourmile Polychrome bowls—which are stylistically, culturally, and temporally related—and place them in a separate category. Actually the use of white as a background for black painted decoration begins in Pinedale Polychrome on bowls and is elaborated in Cedar Creek and Fourmile polychromes on both bowls and jars, where it is particularly prevalent on jar necks. The reasoning I would follow here is that Fourmile Polychrome bowls have no *large* areas of white because they have no necks. The preceding type description has changed Colton and Hargrave's description in that the jars which would necessarily have to be classed as Showlow Polychrome are put back into the same types as their accompanying bowls—Cedar Creek Polychrome, Fourmile Polychrome, and Point of Pines Polychrome. Having a separate category for the jars which belong to these three types is not particularly useful as long as the jars can be separated from each other on much the same basis as the bowls can be separated from each other.

Showlow Polychrome is retained as a type, however, because it not only exhibits a greater use of white than the other closely related types, but also possesses stylistic attributes which are transitional to two other types—Kinishba Polychrome and Showlow Glaze-on-white—and as such, forms a useful taxonomic category.

Summary Description

Showlow Polychrome bowls carry a red slip on their exteriors and either an all white or part white-part red slip on their interiors. Jars have an overall white exterior slip except for the bases which are left red. The paste is light colored with sherd temper. Black glaze paint, sometimes mat red-brown paint, and white paint are used in the decoration. A medium depth bowl with rounded sides and base and walls that incurve at the rim is the most common shape. Small bowls with vertical sides and flattened bottoms, and large jars also occur. Interior decoration on bowls either focuses on the center or goes to the rim. Jars are decorated in banded patterns. Motifs on bowl interiors and jar exteriors are frequently medium width linear units with triangular serrated ends, and are either massed or relatively open in treatment. Large single central figures also occur. Motifs on bowl exteriors consist of either fine white lines or black and white motifs between two wide,

white-bordered, black banding lines as in Fourmile Polychrome. The center of abundance is north of the Salt River between Cherry Creek and the White River below the Mogollon Rim. The time of occurrence is A.D. 1325 to 1400.

POINT OF PINES POLYCHROME

History

Named by: Wasley 1952: 46.
Synonyms: Fourmile Polychrome: Point of Pines variety (Wendorf 1950: 43).
Previous descriptions: Wendorf 1950: 43; Wasley 1952: 46; Gifford 1957: 92; Morris 1957: 20.
Type site: Arizona W:10:51, Point of Pines, Arizona.
Basis of present description: Analysis of 16 whole or restorable vessels in the collection of the Arizona State Museum and Amerind Foundation from Point of Pines; reference to previous descriptions where specified; distribution based on Wasley (1952: 146).

Technology

Construction: Coiling followed by scraping.
Paste: The paste is brown with fine to large angular fragments of leucite tuff and occasionally sand. Golden colored mica is conspicuous in the paste and on the slipped surface. A dark core is common.
Wall thickness: 5 to 8 mm.
Paint: The black varies in appearance from a shiny to a mat glaze, except in worn spots or areas where it was thinly applied, where it is light brown. Frequently it is bright green in oxidized portions suggesting a copper content. The white paint is chalky and fugitive and is probably kaolin.
Application of paint: The white paint is always applied before the black to outline motifs and areas where it remains as a decorative border to black design units.
Surface finish: Bowls are slipped red on both interior and exterior. Jars have either an overall red slip or a red slip on the body and a white slip on the neck and upper shoulders. Neck interiors are slipped the same color as the neck exterior. The surface is rarely well smoothed; usually it is uneven and sometimes lumpy. Bottoms and lower sides are usually very uneven. Pitting is common. Narrow polishing marks are usually present. Crazing is rare to absent. Fire clouds when present are usually large and

FIG. 39. Showlow Polychrome vessels.
- *a.* ASM 23853. Kinishba.
- *b.* ASM A-8655. Point of Pines, Ariz. W:10:50 B.
- *c.* GP-6875. Showlow.
- *d.* ASM 21615. Kinishba.
- *e.* GP-6891. Showlow.
- *f.* ASM 3032. Kinishba.
- *g.* GP-6847. Showlow.

a, c related to Pinedale style; *d,* Fourmile style; *b, e, f,* related to Fourmile and Kinishba styles.
Diameter of *e:* 27.6 cm.

may cover the entire interior of bowls and large portions of the exteriors of bowls and jars.

Slip color: The slip color is red, orange, or red brown: Munsell 10R 5/6, 3 vessels; 10R 5/5, 2 vessels; 10R 4/6, 1 vessel; 5YR 4/6, 2 vessels; 2.5YR 5/5, 2 vessels; 2.5YR 4/6, 1 vessel; 2.5YR 5/4, 1 vessel; 2.5YR 5/6, 1 vessel; 5YR 5/6, 1 vessel; and, undeterminable because of blackening, 2 vessels.

Shapes

Bowls: Bowls are of medium depth with rounded sides and bases and walls that incurve at the rim, 13 examples; dia. 23.0 - 34.0 cm.; ht. 9.5 - 15.0 cm.; incurvature 1 - 6 mm. Rims are rounded, 11 examples; internally beveled, 1 example; or thickened internally with a slight bevel, 1 example.

Jars: Jars are large with high rounded shoulders and short necks that taper inward toward the rim, 3 examples; dia. 25.2 - 31.0 cm.; ht. 20.5 - 24.0 cm.

Painted Decoration

Fields of decoration: All jar necks, jar bodies, bowl interiors, and bowl exteriors bear painted decoration.

Motifs on bowl exteriors: Motifs on bowl exteriors are usually black frets or keys or combinations of these or other black motifs with fine white lines. Fine white lines by themselves occur on only three bowls. Other motifs are: black zigzag bands, black rectilinear birds (Fig. 40 *i*), and black wings opposed by white wings (Fig. 40 *d*). White "F" hooks appear on five bowl exteriors and crosshatched corner angles (Fig. 40 *a*) on one.

Banding lines: All bowls show a broad black banding line with a lower white edge on the interior walls at the rim, even though there is only one banded layout. All three jars show banded layouts with broad black banding lines with one or both borders in white. All except three of the bowl exteriors exhibit two black banding lines in which the upper has a lower white border and the lower has both borders in white. Of the other three, one has simply a narrow white lower banding line, one has no white border on the upper banding line, and one has no lower banding line at all. No line breaks are present.

Line and motif width: Banding lines and uncomplicated portions of linear motifs are generally the same width and range from 7 to 15 mm. With one

exception other framing lines range from 4 to 10 mm. in width and are wider than the hatching lines. In the one exception the hatching and motif framing lines are both 2 mm. wide. The white lines also average 2 mm. in width.

Style: Point of Pines Polychrome is decorated in a degenerate version of Fourmile style. A few vessels (Fig. 41*b*) show artistry comparable to that on Fourmile Polychrome, but they are the exception. Patterns are usually not only poorly conceived, but poorly applied, and are usually ill adapted to the field of decoration and leave either large undecorated spaces or massed units crammed into a small area.

Spatial Distribution

Point of Pines Polychrome has been found at 18 sites near Point of Pines, Arizona and at a few sites on Nantack Ridge which rises just to the south of Point of Pines (Wasley 1952: 146).

Temporal Distribution

Point of Pines Polychrome is limited to the Point of Pines Phase which has been tentatively dated at A.D. 1400 to 1450. There are no tree-ring dates for this phase. The beginning date is based on the disappearance of Fourmile Polychrome by approximately A.D. 1400. The few sherds of Fourmile Polychrome found in Point of Pines Phase contexts seem logically to be intrusive from earlier trash (see discussion in Wasley 1952: 123). I have reclassified one partial vessel as Point of Pines Polychrome which Wasley (1952, Pl. 16) originally classified as Fourmile Polychrome. This vessel exhibits design treatment comparable to that of Point of Pines Polychrome, and there is golden mica in the paste. The paste itself is dark gray rather than brown which I think is probably the result of firing. The terminal date for the Point of Pines Phase is based on the absence of post-A.D. 1450 intrusive Hopi and Zuni tradewares (Morris 1957: 54 *a*).

Discussion

Point of Pines Polychrome is considered to be a type separate from Fourmile Polychrome, although it is closely related. It occupies a time span largely separate from that of Fourmile Polychrome and has distinctive attributes in paste, temper, and design treatment. Also, it may represent the diffusion of the Fourmile style of design to a group which did not

a

b

c

d

e

f

g

h

i

◄■■ **FIG. 40.** Point of Pines Polychrome bowls.

a. ASM A-15597. Ariz. W:10:50 B, rm. 8, floor fill. Design partially restored.

b. ASM A-15577. Ariz. W:10:50 B, rm. 5, floor fill.

c. ASM A-17106. Ariz. W:10:50 B. Design partially restored.

d. ASM A-10346. Ariz. W:10:52. Design partially restored.

e. ASM A-15576. Ariz. W:10:50 B, rm. 5, floor fill.

f. ASM A-8496. Ariz. W:10:50 A, rm. 6, floor.

g. ASM A-6144. Ariz. W:10:51, floor rms. 12 and 13.

h. ASM A-15578. Ariz. W:10:50 B, rm. 5, floor fill.

i. ASM A-15579. Ariz. W:10:50 B, rm. 5, floor fill.

All are degenerate Fourmile style.

Diameter of *h*: 24.0 cm.

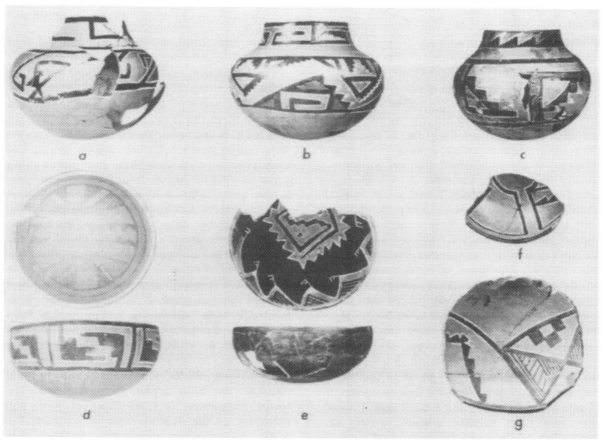

FIG. 41. Point of Pines Polychrome bowls and jars.

a. ASM A-6602. Ariz. W:10:47, Kiva 1, floor.

b. ASM A-15491. Ariz. W:10:50 B, rm. 6, floor.

c. ASM A-16467. Ariz. W:10:105, rm. 1, floor 1.

d. AF 1816. Ariz. W:10:51, rm. 21.

e. ASM A-16698. Ariz. W:10:50 B, rm. 10, floor 1. Design partially restored.

f. ASM A-4517. Ariz. W:10:51.

g. ASM UNCAT. Ariz. W:10:51, rm. 13, floor.

b, good Fourmile style; remainder degenerate Fourmile style.

Diameter of *a*: 31.0 cm.

previously make painted pottery. Some vessels of Pinedale Polychrome, Cedar Creek Polychrome, and Fourmile Polychrome which have a brown paste with golden mica inclusions have been found at Point of Pines. Unlike Point of Pines Polychrome, which also has this type of paste, these vessels do not exhibit the distinctively poor artistry and design which characterize Point of Pines Polychrome. It is uncertain whether they were made at Point of Pines or in some other area where the residual clays are much the same. They are, however, potential candidates as Point of Pines varieties of their respective types. Studies of their temper have not been made, but should it turn out that it is leucite tuff it would seem even more likely that they were locally-made varieties: Point of Pines Polychrome would then be a late degenerate version of these varieties.

Summary Description

Point of Pines Polychrome bowls are slipped red, orange, or reddish brown on the interior and exterior. Jars have either an overall red slip on their exterior and neck interior or a red slip on the body and a white slip on the neck and upper shoulders. The paste is brown with specks of golden mica and crushed rock (leucite tuff) temper. The paint is a black or mat glaze which has sometimes turned green. In places where it was thinly applied it appears as a thin dark stain rather than as a glaze. Medium depth bowls with rounded sides and bases and walls that incurve at the rim are the most common forms, but large jars also occur. Interior decoration on bowls usually focuses on the center, but frequently continues up the interior walls almost to the rim. The rim band itself is a broad black band with a lower white border. Motifs on bowl interiors are either large central figures, sectors spaced by background areas, or circles with internal fillers. In treatment designs on bowl interiors and jar exteriors range from relatively open spaces with few painted units to massed treatment with a lot of decoration squeezed into a small area. Frequent filler motifs are negative stepped figures, dots, stepped line fillers, white "F" hooks, and rectangles with parallel hatching. Designs on bowl exteriors consist of fine white lines or of black units outlined in white between two heavy black banding lines. Jars also bear banded layouts. Most black motifs have one or both edges outlined in white which is applied before the black. Hatching is not common, but when it occurs it is usually parallel. Line work and layout are usually poorly designed and poorly executed. The

type is found only in the vicinity of Point of Pines, Arizona, during the Point of Pines Phase, A.D. 1400 to 1450.

HESHOTA POLYCHROME, HESHOTA BLACK-ON-RED, KWAKINA POLYCHROME

Summary Description

Summary descriptions for these three pottery types are based on Woodbury and Woodbury (1966), Rinaldo (1959, 1961), Reed (1955), Martin and Willis (1940), Kidder and Shepard (1936), Stubbs and Stallings (1953), and examination of sherds and several vessels in the collection of the Arizona State Museum. The names and dates employed for these types are those used by the Woodburys.

Heshota (Heshotauthla) Polychrome vessels are slipped red on the interior and exterior of bowls and dippers and red on the exterior of jars. The most common shape for bowls is a medium depth with rounded bases and walls that incurve at the rim. The paste is light gray to buff with angular temper. The black paint is a good thick shiny glaze with a strong copper content (Shephard 1942: 223) and sometimes appears green. White paint is used on bowl exteriors in continuous or unit patterns which resemble those in St. Johns Polychrome, but which employ lines which are only about 3 mm. wide. White does not appear on bowl interiors. Black may also appear on the exteriors of bowls in conjunction with white in which case it is applied after the white. Black is used on bowl exteriors either to form panel dividers in an essentially white pattern, as in Springerville Polychrome, or occasionally to form unit motifs which are outlined in white, as in Pinedale Polychrome. Bowl interiors are decorated in either Tularosa style or in a style similar to Pinedale style, but less complex. The latter appears to predominate. The spatial distribution is from Point of Pines and Bidahochi on the west to Pecos on the east. The center of distribution is probably the Cibola area where the Woodburys found it common between El Morro and Zuni. The estimated time period is A.D. 1300 to 1375.

Heshota Black-on-red is the same as Heshota Polychrome except that white is lacking in the color scheme.

Kwakina Polychrome appears to be the same thing as Heshota Polychrome except that bowls have a complete or partial white slip on the interior. The black paint is a glaze. Bowls retain the red slip color on the exterior, and are decorated in either narrow white line motifs or more frequently black unit motifs outlined in white. Rinaldo (1961, Fig. 95) reports some sherds of Kwakina with red motifs contrasted to the slip on bowl exteriors. The style of design on bowl interiors is either Tularosa or a style similar to Pinedale, but much less elaborate. The latter appears to predominate. A Kwakina bowl with Tularosa style on the interior is illustrated in Figure 25 *g*. The area of distribution is from at least El Morro on the east to Kinishba on the west. Rinaldo (1961: 134) estimates the temporal duration of the type as A.D. 1300 to 1375.

3. DESIGN STYLES

Design styles on ceramics have received a fair amount of consideration in the Southwest. Amsden's (1936) work on Hohokam styles is a classic as is Mera's (1939) monograph on historic style trends. Colton's (1953: 46) styles—Lino, Kana-a, Black Mesa, Sosi, Dogoszhi, Flagstaff, Kayenta, and Tularosa—are recognized by most Southwestern archaeologists. Other styles are recognized verbally, but have never been formally defined. All Southwestern painted pottery is interrelated to a degree, and gradual transitions both in space and time can be seen as one proceeds upward in the temporal scale and laterally from region to region. The various cultural subareas of the Southwest had in effect ceramic co-traditions which mutually influenced one another through the usual channels of diffusion, and occasionally became more intimately associated through actual population movements. Widespread similarities in ceramic styles were one of the results of such influence. Stylistic analysis, however, tends to emphasize the differences between ceramic styles both temporally and spatially rather than the overall similarities. Some stylistic attributes remained comparatively static, whereas others changed rapidly. The latter are basic to the definitions of particular styles as they indicate change and it is through the use of indicators such as these that archaeologists build cultural sequences. Stylistic attributes are also important if they cluster in a particular area and are rare to absent in another area which was occupied simultaneously. In such cases they are inferred to be indicative of important cultural differences. It is frequently necessary, however, to use concepts and abstractions in defining sequent styles in one subarea that would be of little use in another subarea. In the White Mountain Redwares, the composition of motifs and the way in which motifs of varying composition are combined on a given field of decoration are of basic importance in understanding stylistic changes within the tradition. Other important attributes of style are color patterns, motifs, layouts, foci of decoration, and artistry as they combine to form a generalized picture of the decoration on these groups of related objects. These terms and several others require a brief explanation.

Field of decoration: The potential field of decoration is the entire surface of a vessel. This potential field is bounded by the limits of the vessel, and is divided further by the structural lines of the vessel. Those fields which are formed by structural boundaries are bowl interiors, bowl exteriors, jar bodies, jar necks, exteriors of narrow-mouthed effigy vessels, rims, and handles. If these areas were used for decoration they are called fields of decoration. On jar exteriors the structural boundary between the neck and the body was sometimes ignored and the whole exterior was treated as one field.

Focus of decoration: The focus of decoration is that portion of the field on which painted motifs are concentrated. *This concept is limited to the discussion of designs on bowl interiors.* Three types of foci are found: (1) *Walls* - in which the walls are painted wholly or in part and decoration goes clear to the rim, but the center of the bowl was left without decoration, except in a few instances where a small filler motif occupies this area (see Fig. 5 b). (2) *Whole field* - the entire bowl interior, including the center and walls to the rim, was used; and (3) *Center* - the decoration appears on the center of the bowl and the walls are bare. It is frequently difficult to observe these different foci from photographs as the incurvature at the rim of bowls sometimes conceals a good part of the wall. Idealized examples of the different foci on bowl interiors with their respective layouts are illustrated in Figure 42.

Layout: The layout is the manner in which the field of decoration is organized. The layout separates the decorated from the undecorated portion of the field, and may, in addition, section the decorated area with a network of lines or spaces. In some instances the boundaries of motifs are the only structural lines present. Idealized layouts are shown in Figure 42. Some variations have not been included. For example, in some St. Johns Polychrome bowls an undecorated star-shaped area rather than an open circle appears in the bottom of the bowl's interior. This was accomplished simply by leaving off the lower banding line. Similarly the upper banding line was sometimes left off on banded layouts and the rim alone served to enclose the upper edge of the band.

Layouts on jar bodies are almost invariably banded. Layouts on bowl exteriors are either continuous motifs with or without banding lines, unit motifs, units pendant from a rim band, or combinations of these.

Motif: Motif is the term used to describe the use to which various units of design are put. Primary motifs are those combinations of design units which are the strongest units in the pattern and which form the basis thereof. Filler motifs are those units which are either included within the boundaries or appended to the borders of a primary motif, or are used to fill an area within the field of decoration which is not covered by the primary motifs. Motifs are described in terms of form and composition. For instance, they may be linear, globular, or triangular in form, and, in composition, solid, hatched, negative or in combinations thereof. The most common units used to form motifs are frets, scrolls, stepped or terraced units, and sectors. Frets are rectilinear units made up of lines joined at an angle and are characterized by length rather than by volume. Scrolls are essentially the same thing except that they are curvilinear rather than rectilinear. Either may be elaborated by stepping or barbing the edges or ends. Stepped or terraced units are for the most part triangles or diamonds which have their exteriors stepped as in a terrace. A sector is a division of a circle formed by two radii and the arc of the circle. These and other units are combined in various manners to form motifs. One of the most common methods of combining units is by interlocking. Interlocking is used in two senses in this paper: (1) where the ends of linear units embrace each other as in a series of interlocked scrolls, and (2) where units with complicated edges oppose and embrace each other like the cogs of a wheel. Units may also be combined by joining or enclosing them within a boundary line.

Color pattern: This term refers to the number of colors used on vessels by field. For example, a Pinedale Polychrome bowl may be black and red on the interior and black-and-white-on-red on the exterior, or it may be black-and-white-on-red on the interior and black and red on the exterior, or all three colors may occur on both fields on the same vessel.

Hatching: Hatching refers to a group of fine lines used to fill a space. It is contrasted to solid in which a space is filled with paint, and to negative in which a space is outlined and background forms the design unit. Four types of hatching are found on this ware: (1) parallel hatching wherein the hatching lines parallel their framing lines or their longest framing line (Fig. 5 *a*); (2) diagonal hatching in which the hatching lines cross from one framing line to the other and do not parallel their longest framing line (Fig. 8 *n*); (3) crosshatching in which the hatching lines cross each other (Fig. 33 *g*); and (4) zigzag hatching in which the hatching lines move in parallel zigzags (Fig. 8 *o*).

Framing lines: A framing line is a line that encloses a motif or a group of motifs. The following specific types of framing lines are referred to in this study: (1) banding line- the framing line enclosing a banded layout; this includes an upper banding line or rim line, and a lower banding line or base line. This term is also used for the band just below the rim on the interior of Fourmile Polychrome bowls which is a retention of this trait after banded layouts have gone out of use; and (2) double banding line - a line actually enclosing the banded layout, but opposed by a separate heavy banding line (Fig. 27 *l*).

Line and motif width: Measurements are given for the width of certain lines and linear design units in the type descriptions. When generalizing about variations among these attributes, narrow refers to widths of 1 to 3 mm., medium to widths of 4 to 7 mm., and wide to widths of 8 to 15 mm. or more.

Pattern: Patterns describe the interplay of primary motifs within the field of decoration. Primary motifs may be joined to each other, interlocked with each other, or separated from each other. The same motif may be repeated, may alternate with another motif of equal strength, or there may be only one primary motif present. Motifs which are repeated and which join or interlock with each other throughout the area of decoration form continuous patterns, whereas separated motifs form sectioned patterns. Continuous patterns exhibit flow or movement whereas sectioned patterns do not. The movement may be either primarily horizontal or vertical. Not all patterns which lack formal sectioning are continuous, however. Design units may interlock to form motifs which oppose one another without interlocking and without formal separation by layout lines or spaces. In general, patterns can be described in terms of whether they are continuous or sectioned; whether motifs are repeated, alternating, or single unit; and whether repetition or alternation is on a horizontal or vertical axis.

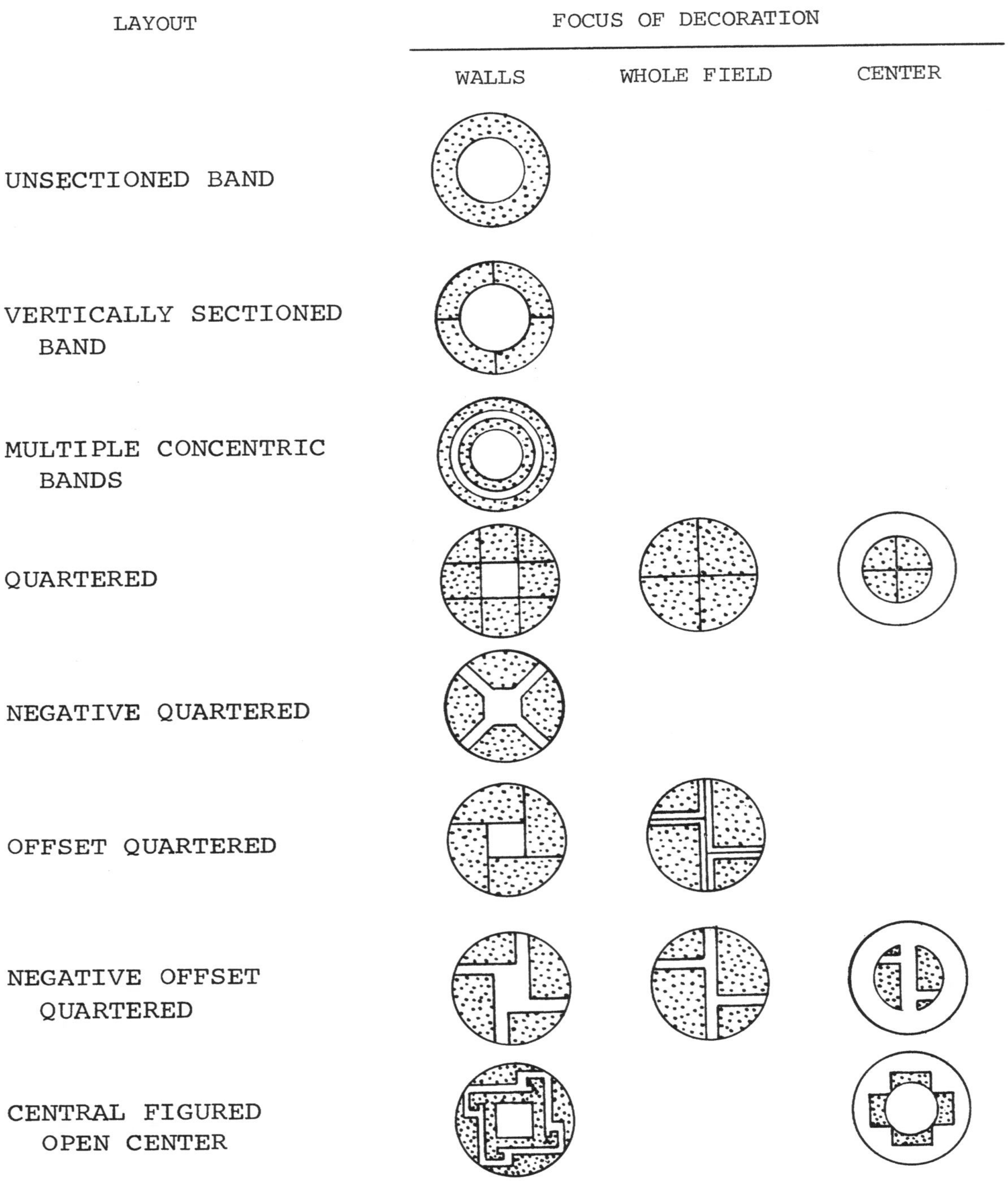

86

LAYOUT	FOCUS OF DECORATION		
	WALLS	WHOLE FIELD	CENTER
UNSECTIONED BAND			
VERTICALLY SECTIONED BAND			
MULTIPLE CONCENTRIC BANDS			
QUARTERED			
NEGATIVE QUARTERED			
OFFSET QUARTERED			
NEGATIVE OFFSET QUARTERED			
CENTRAL FIGURED OPEN CENTER			

FIG. 42. Idealized layouts found in White Mountain Redware.

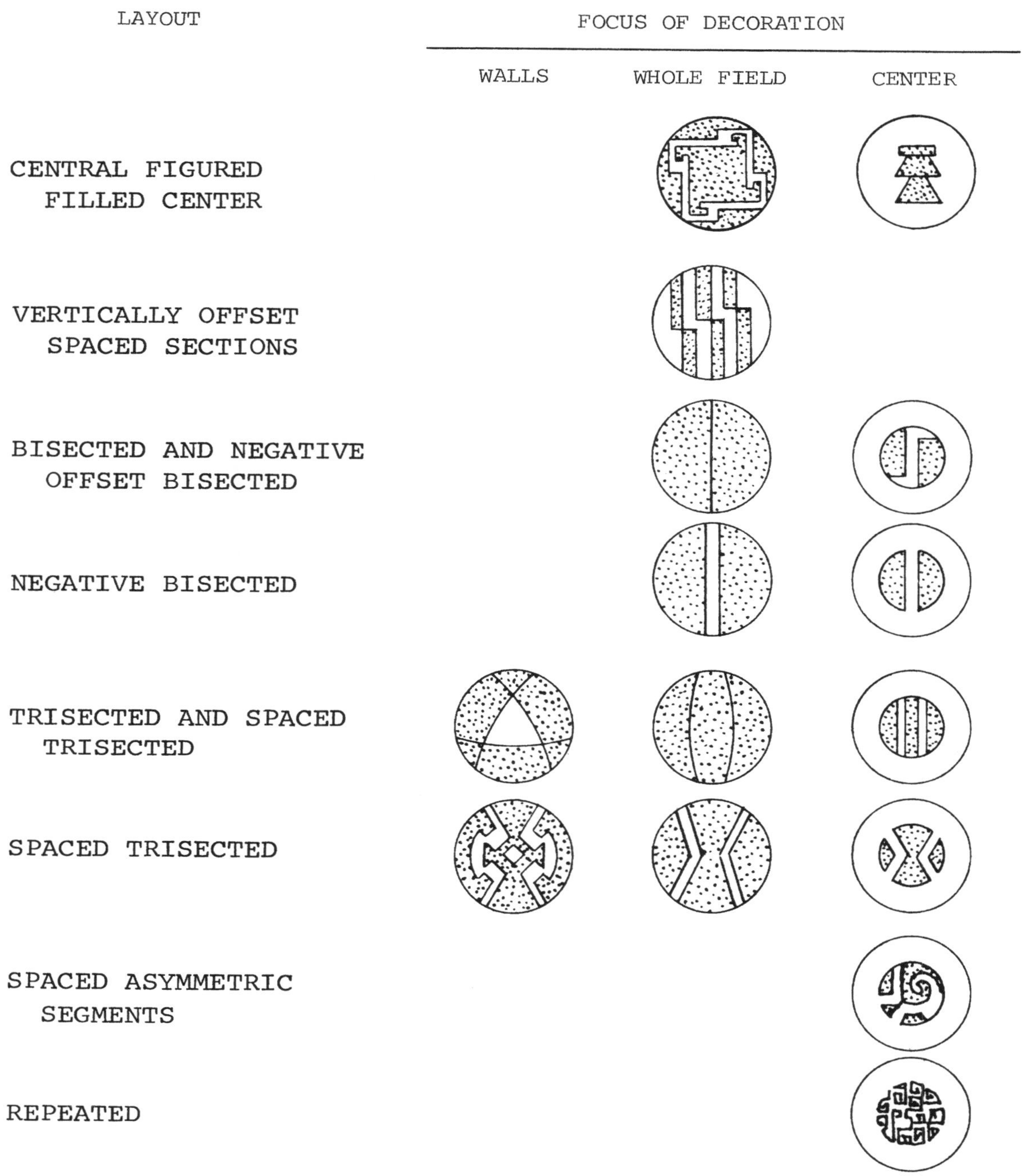

LAYOUT	FOCUS OF DECORATION		
	WALLS	WHOLE FIELD	CENTER
CENTRAL FIGURED FILLED CENTER			
VERTICALLY OFFSET SPACED SECTIONS			
BISECTED AND NEGATIVE OFFSET BISECTED			
NEGATIVE BISECTED			
TRISECTED AND SPACED TRISECTED			
SPACED TRISECTED			
SPACED ASYMMETRIC SEGMENTS			
REPEATED			

FIG. 42. (Cont.)   Idealized layouts found in White Mountain Redware.

FIG. 43. Holbrook style. Hatched design units do not appear.

Artistry: Artistry refers to standards of brush work and technique.

White Mountain Redware first appeared during late Pueblo II in the Cibola area. It climaxed during Pueblo IV in the Mogollon Rim area, and by Pueblo V had been superseded by types with other color patterns. During the course of its history six partly sequent and developmentally related styles of design are found on examples of this pottery. The same styles are found on black-on-white pottery indigenous to the same areas. These styles are: (1) Holbrook; (2) Puerco; (3) Wingate; (4) Tularosa; (5) Pinedale; and (6) Fourmile. These styles apply to the interior decoration on bowls and to the exterior decoration on jars and not to other fields. Color pattern is not a diagnostic for any of these styles, and as such the styles cross cut the black-on-red, black-on-white, and polychrome divisions which are basic to the formulation of pottery types. The types of exterior decoration on bowls have not been given style names.

HOLBROOK STYLE

Holbrook style is differentiated from other pottery styles by the presence of *solid motifs only* on the field of decoration. Hatching does not occur on

vessels decorated in this style. The typical motifs are joined or interlocked ribbon-like frets with either plain or barbed ends in symmetrical arrangements. Dots appended to these frets are common. Other elaborations are absent. Layouts are almost invariably banded and on bowl interiors the decoration focuses on the walls. Double banding lines are absent and frets are of medium width. This style is in effect transitional between Sosi and Black Mesa styles (Colton 1953: 46), on the one hand, and Puerco style, on the other, and embodies stylistic attributes common to all three styles. Artistry is good but the total effect is repetitive and uninteresting. In White Mountain Redware, Holbrook style is found only on Puerco Black-on-red. Black-on-white types which are decorated in this style are Holbrook Black-on-white (Colton 1955, Ware 9B - Type 2) and Puerco Black-on-white in part. It may also prove to be common on Escavada Black-on-white. The style is basically late Pueblo II and early Pueblo III and dates from about A.D. 1000 to 1150.

PUERCO STYLE

Puerco style is distinguishable from other styles by the presence on the same field of either solid and

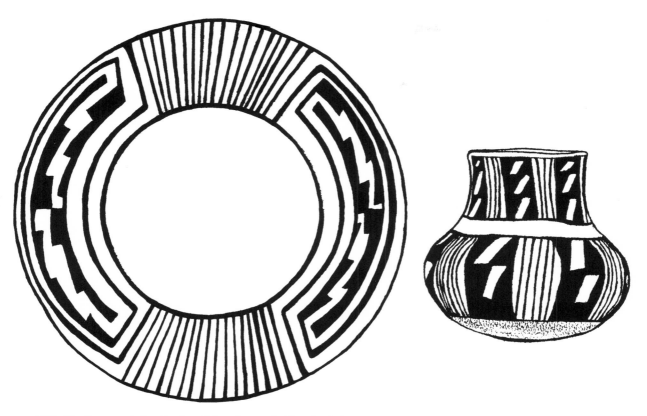

FIG. 44. Puerco style. Both solid and parallel-hatched design units appear on the same field in Puerco style, but do not interlock. Checkerboards instead of parallel-hatched units are frequently found.

hatched motifs which *do not interlock with each other* or solid and checkerboard motifs with no hatched units present. (Checkerboards could actually be classified as a type of hatching.) Hatched motifs are invariably made up of parallel lines. Layouts are with few exceptions either vertically sectioned bands or multiple concentric bands in which either parallel-hatched units or checkerboard units alternate with solid units. The latter are usually frets although rectangles composed of solid and negative bars are also common. Patterns are symmetrical. Pendant dots, negative diamonds and zigzags, and barbed ends to frets are present. Bowls have a wall focus of decoration. Framing lines are the same width as hatching lines, and frets are of medium width. Double banding lines are absent. The effect is repetitive and dull. The style is named after Puerco Black-on-white and certainly reflects what Gladwin (1931: 24-6) had in mind when he separated the vessels of this type from the other black-on-whites in the Scorse collection. In the White Mountain Redwares this style is common on Puerco Black-on-red and occasionally appears on Wingate Polychrome, St. Johns Black-on-

red, St. Johns Polychrome, and Pinedale Polychrome. It is the most common style on Puerco Black-on-white and probably occasionally appears on other black-on-white types. The style is frequent in late Pueblo II and early Pueblo III from about A.D. 1000 to 1200 but probably lingers on as a rarity for another 75 years or so.

WINGATE STYLE

In Wingate style motifs are made up of interlocked solid and hatched units in which the hatched units are always much wider than the corresponding solid units. This treatment of the motifs is the diagnostic attribute of Wingate style. Edges of motifs are most frequently barbed although plain and stepped edges also occur. Diagonal hatching is preponderant although parallel-hatched panel dividers are occasionally found. Banded layouts on all vessels and a wall focus of decoration on bowls are typical and most common, but central figured layouts which sometimes cover the whole of the bowl interior and do not leave the center open are also common and typical. Frequent motifs are barbed frets and barbed scrolls

FIG. 45. Wingate style. Wide diagonally-hatched design units interlocked
with medium width solid units typify Wingate style.

either repeated in continuous patterns or in swastika-like central figured arrangements. Dots and negative circles with dots are common filler motifs. Framing lines and hatching lines are the same width. Patterns are symmetrical and artistry is generally good. The overall stylistic picture is one of wide units with complicated edges composed of fine line diagonal hatching, balanced and interlocked with medium width solid units in either a banded or central figured layout. Wingate style is common on Wingate Black-on-red and on early Wingate Polychrome and occasionally appears on St. Johns Polychrome. It is also the common decorative style of Reserve Black-on-white and is certainly close if not identical to the style found on Gallup Black-on-white. One of the decorative styles of Mesa Verde Black-on-white is also closely related and is, I suspect, the earlier of the main Mesa Verde styles. Wingate style is common from about A.D. 1000 to 1200.

TULAROSA STYLE

Tularosa style is characterized by some attributes common to both Puerco and Wingate styles. One of these attributes is the interaction of design units on bowl interiors and jar bodies in which a wide hatched

unit with complicated edges is interlocked with a medium width solid unit of approximately the same form. The motifs formed in this manner are closely massed and are usually repeated six or eight times in a banded layout. Decoration focuses on the bowl walls and the center is always open. Occasionally the band is sectioned by parallel-hatched panel dividers or by other panel dividers and relationships with Puerco style are indicated. Other types of interaction also occur—motifs composed of joined solid and hatched units are interlocked, or motifs composed of both solid and hatched units alternate with bands of parallel hatching. Hatching is parallel as in Puerco style, diagonal as in Wingate style, or mixed. The hatched portions of interlocked solid and hatched motifs are narrower than in Wingate style, but are still wider than the solid units. This permits a greater number of them to be repeated on the field. Artistry is generally mediocre, occasionally very good. White is sometimes used to outline black motifs. Motifs more frequently have stepped rather than barbed ends or edges and the rather wide pointed barb typical of Wingate style is rare. Scrolls, double terraces, frets with stepped ends, and vertical zigzags are typical motifs. Framing lines are the same width

FIG. 46. Tularosa style. Massed joined or interlocked solid and hatched design units are characteristic. Hatched units are narrower than in Wingate style.

as hatching lines. Double banding lines are rarely present. Patterns are symmetrical. Tularosa style is the most common style on St. Johns Polychrome, St. Johns Black-on-red, Springerville Polychrome, and late Wingate Polychrome; it appears less frequently on Pinedale Polychrome, Pinedale Black-on-red, Kwakina Polychrome, and Heshota Polychrome. Tularosa style is also the most common style on Tularosa Black-on-white, and I suspect is present on Pinedale Black-on-white. Tularosa style was common from about A.D. 1200 to 1300 during late Pueblo III and may well have lasted even later in the heart of the Zuni country.

PINEDALE STYLE

Pinedale style is a transitional style very closely related, on the one hand, to Tularosa style and, on the other, to Fourmile style. As in Tularosa style the most common layout is still an unsectioned band, and the focus of decoration is still usually the walls of bowls. There is a major change, however, in that the decoration now frequently focuses on the whole interior of many bowls. The decoration never focuses on the center as in Fourmile style. Also, as in Tularosa style, motifs composed of interlocked solid and hatched units are common, but these units are

larger than in Tularosa style, the solid unit is as wide as the hatched one and consequently stands out from the field, and with few exceptions the motifs are repeated no more than four times. There is also a trend toward broadening and elaborating what were formerly layout lines into motifs, and in using negative layouts. The edges of linear motifs still show complicated steps and barbs, but internal elaboration of large triangular, curvilinear, and rectilinear motifs using dots, dotted lines, parallel lines, and particularly squiggled lines becomes common. Double banding lines are frequent. Frets and scrolls are still common motifs, but the double terrace motif which is very frequent in Tularosa style no longer appears. Small pendant bird or parrot figures made by adding a curved beak, legs, and a tail to a triangle are typical. The running diamond motif (Fig. 55) makes its appearance in Pinedale style and is not found earlier in White Mountain Redwares. Patterns are symmetrical and are formed of either alternating or repeated motifs. Framing lines are usually the same width as hatching lines, but on some Cedar Creek Polychrome vessels they are twice as wide as the framing lines. White is frequently used to outline black motifs. The artistry is generally excellent. Pinedale style is transitional between Tularosa and Fourmile styles in the

FIG. 47. Pinedale style. Superior artistry, bold treatment, and the whole field focus of decoration, as well as the center focus, are typical of Pinedale style.

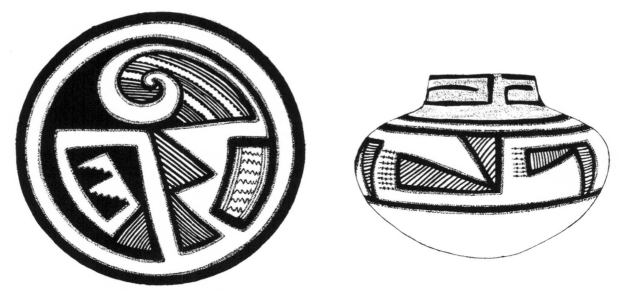

FIG. 48. Fourmile style. The center focus of decoration on bowls, heavy framing lines, and the asymmetry of some layouts separate Fourmile style from all earlier styles.

trends toward superior artistry, greater elaboration of motifs, boldness, the whole field focus of decoration which is transitional to the center focus, increased use of double banding lines, and the trend away from interlocked solid and hatched units with complicated edges toward internal elaboration of motifs using

filler devices. Pinedale style appears on Pinedale Polychrome, Pinedale Black-on-red, Cedar Creek Polychrome, and occasionally on St. Johns Polychrome. Some Heshota Polychrome vessels exhibit many of the features of Pinedale style, particularly the squiggled line fillers and running diamond motifs,

FIG. 49. Changes in, and developments from, scrolls in sequent styles of White Mountain Redware.

but lack the excellent artistry, the use of white outlining on motifs, the whole field focus of decoration, and the general elaboration of motifs. In general they retain the features of St. Johns style to a greater extent. Glaze I Red (Kidder and Shepard 1936) exhibits some features of Pinedale style, particularly the squiggled line fillers, double banding lines, small parrots, and running diamond motif. White outlining, the whole field focus of decoration on bowls, and general elaboration of motifs are absent, however. Pinedale style and variations of it (not specifically included within Pinedale style) ushered in Pueblo IV in various parts of the Southwest at or close to A.D. 1300. The style itself was elaborated during the following century, but even before A.D. 1400 it probably declined in popularity in the Mogollon Rim area as Fourmile style developed and became increasingly popular.

FOURMILE STYLE

Fourmile style represents a radical departure from earlier styles in that there was a change of focus of decoration on bowl interiors from the walls to the center. Large single units are admirably adapted to the latter area of decoration whereas multiple repeated units are well adapted to bowl walls. The layouts found on bowls with a whole interior focus of decoration in Pinedale style continued into Fourmile style, but sectioned only the bowl centers. Fourmile style also differs from preceding styles in that many layouts lack bilateral symmetry. Much of Fourmile design on bowl interiors was based on sectioning a circle into multiple units after which either like units were repeated or unlike units alternated. Asymmetric patterns resulted when this circle was sectioned into unlike units. The sectioning itself was usually done by spacing. Jars and "flower pots" retained banded layouts and this type of layout is certainly best suited to their respective shapes. Most motifs are black and have white outlines. Another attribute in which Fourmile style differs from preceding styles is in the non-interlocking of design units to form motifs. Units with complicated edges do not oppose and interlock with a similarly shaped unit. Internal elaboration of primary motifs using parallel-hatched units, stepped line fillers, negative stepped units, dots, and occasionally patches of white, was the rule. Fourmile style also departs from earlier styles in that large biomorphic figures first appear commonly on White Mountain Redware. These figures appear to gradually develop from geometric units. Scrolls which suddenly sprouted tail feathers and gradually changed into large birds (Fig. 49) show this transition best. Purely geometric motifs are still the most common units of design, but the development of life forms is a radical change from previous styles. Wide framing lines which are always wider than hatching lines enclose all motifs. Even though bowls no longer have banded layouts, they still retain a broad band just below the interior rim. Artistry is good to excellent with the exception of Point of Pines Polychrome on which it is generally incredibly bad. Fourmile style is found on Fourmile Polychrome, Showlow Polychrome, and Kinishba Polychrome. It lasted from about A.D. 1300 to 1400 in its main form and for about an additional 50 years in a degenerate form on Point of Pines Polychrome.

4. CHANGE AND CONTINUITY
IN WHITE MOUNTAIN REDWARE

White Mountain Redware is merely one segment of the entire Southwestern tradition of painted ceramics. The earliest known Southwestern pottery appears in Mogollon contexts about 250 B.C. (Martin and others 1952) and consists of both slipped redware and unslipped brownware. Both Hohokam and later Mogollon ceramics seem to be related to these earliest wares which in turn possibly have their origin in Mesoamerica (Jennings 1956: 78-82). The beginnings of Anasazi ceramics are still not clear, but one would suspect that they originated under stimulus from the Mogollon by A.D. 500, and rapidly developed their distinctive Lino style in black-on-white with motifs taken over for the most part from basketry decoration. The Anasazi also began to manufacture redware at a comparatively early date with the appearance of Abajo Red-on-orange by about A.D. 700, followed by Bluff and La Plata black-on-reds by about 800 (Abel 1955). The relationships of these types, if any, to the Mogollon redware tradition is obscure. Neither the early Mogollon nor Anasazi redware types are found localized in the Cibola area, however, where during the eleventh century White Mountain Redware began to be made.

The archaeological record for the Cibola area shows the emergence of redware during late Pueblo II in the shapes and styles of the indigenous black-on-white types, the rapid development of polychrome during early Pueblo III, the replacement of black-on-white by polychrome and black-on-red during late Pueblo III and early Pueblo IV, and the eventual replacement of redware by types with a light background color during late Pueblo IV. The major breaks between both styles and types and the expansion of the tradition to the Mogollon Rim and Rio Grande areas as well as its eventual decline occurred at the times of known major cultural discontinuities in various regions of the Southwest. The following paragraphs summarize the prehistory of the Cibola area, and indicate the trends in painted ceramics.

LA PLATA PHASE

The earliest cultural phase for the area is the La Plata Phase which lasted from about A.D. 400 to 700

at a Basketmaker III stage of development. La Plata Black-on-white was the predominant if not the only painted type (Wasley 1960: 36). Within the Cibola area on the time level of the La Plata Phase were certain other cultural assemblages which suggest that people other than the Anasazi were also in the region. Near Lupton, Arizona, Wasley (1960) reports Mogollon brownware in pit house associations almost to the exclusion of Anasazi pottery of the same time period. In the Petrified Forest National Monument, the Flattop Site (Wendorf 1953) exhibits traits of Anasazi, Mogollon, and possibly Hohokam. The paddle and anvil pottery there is in marked contrast to both Mogollon and Anasazi pottery. Non-Anasazi culture patterns later than these have not appeared in the archaeological record and the Cibola area continued in the Anasazi pattern throughout the remainder of its prehistory, although certain traits incorporated into the pattern seem likely to have been of Mogollon derivation (Wheat 1955: 205-30).

WHITE MOUND PHASE

The White Mound Phase has been documented for both the southern part of the region at the Twin Butte site (Wendorf 1953) and Kiatuthlanna (Roberts 1931), and in the northern part of the area at White Mound (Gladwin 1945: 11-27) and Arizona K:12:8 (Wasley 1960: 36-7). The indigenous decorated pottery was White Mound Black-on-white, but redware was also present in limited quantities. At White Mound, Gladwin notes polished redware with black interiors and San Francisco Red of Mogollon origin from the floor fill of the pit houses, and Tusayan Black-on-red from northeastern Arizona in the later fill. At Kiatuthlanna (Roberts 1931: 120), pottery with a fugitive red wash occurs, but it is uncertain whether it belongs to the White Mound Phase or to later components at that site. At the Twin Butte site sherds or vessels of Lino Red (Tallahogan Red), Forestdale Red, Woodruff Red, and Forestdale Black-on-red were recovered. Pit house dwellings with surface storage structures characterize the architectural remains associated with this late Basketmaker III Phase which dates from about A.D. 700 to 800.

KIATUTHLANNA PHASE

The Kiatuthlanna Phase follows the White Mound Phase and is dated from A.D. 800 to 875 (Wasley 1959, Fig. 25). Components have been excavated at Kiatuthlanna (Roberts 1931), in the Whitewater area near Allentown (Roberts 1939, 1940), and at White Mound and Red Mesa (Gladwin 1945: 41-8). The most abundant painted pottery type is Kiatuthlanna Black-on-white. Redware is rare although Gladwin notes polished redware, and some of Roberts' (1940: 42-3, 50-1) "early Developmental Pueblo black on red" could belong in this phase. Dwellings consisted of pit houses and some surface structures which were at a Pueblo I stage of development.

RED MESA PHASE

Excavated sites of the Red Mesa Phase are known only from the northern fringe of the Cibola area. The Red Mesa Phase, originally defined by Gladwin (1945: 49-63), has recently been divided into an early and a late Red Mesa Phase (Olson and Wasley 1956: 258; Wendorf and Lehmer 1956: 195). The Phase as a whole dates from approximately A.D. 875 to 1000 (Wasley 1959, Fig. 25). The principal excavated sites of the early Red Mesa Phase are LA 2508 (Wendorf and Lehmer 1956: 192), LA 2655, and LA 2701 (Olson and Wasley 1956: 325, 377-90). Late Red Mesa Phase sites are LA 2700 (Olson and Wasley 1956: 375-6) and some sites known only from surface survey (Wendorf and Lehmer 1956: 192). Gladwin's Red Mesa Phase components also belong in this phase as do parts of the excavations near Allentown (Roberts 1939, 1940), and some additional components near Lupton recently reported by Wasley (1960: 37-8). The principal decorated pottery was Red Mesa Black-on-white. Redware was probably present in minor amounts, as Gladwin (1945: 57) reports a few sherds of red pottery with rectilinear designs in faded brown paint on a polished red surface, and several sherds of polished redware with black interiors. Roberts' "early Developmental Pueblo black on red" may be the same thing as Gladwin reports. One sherd of fugitive red at LA 2700 and a few of polished red with smudged interior at LA 2701 are reported by Olson and Wasley (1956: 389). The ceramics added to Red Mesa Black-on-white, which serve to differentiate the late Red Mesa Phase from the early, are Gallup Black-on-white and Puerco Black-on-white, at least the Escavada variety

(Olson and Wasley 1956: 258). The stage of development was Pueblo II with small surface dwellings and some pit houses.

WINGATE PHASE

The Wingate Phase is known from a number of excavated sites. The pueblo horizon at Kiatuthlanna (Roberts 1931) belongs to this phase. Components at Wingate 11:53, Wingate 11:20, and Wingate 11:24 (Gladwin 1945: 67-77) are part of it also. LA 2699, LA 2640, and most of LA 2639 (Olson and Wasley 1956: 292-374) are also included. Unit 3 of Roberts' (1939: 277) excavations near Allentown may also belong to this phase as Gladwin (1945: 76) suggests, although the less than 0.2 per cent of red pottery from Roberts' whole excavation—which could include Wingate Black-on-red, Puerco Black-on-red, and other redware—cannot be tied into any definite portion of the excavation. Additional Wingate Phase excavations have been reported by Wasley (1960: 38-9) near Lupton to which the previously cited tree-ring dates belong (see Wingate Black-on-red, temporal distribution). Architecture consisted of small surface masonry pueblos with contiguous rooms facing a plaza with a kiva, and apparently pit houses (Wasley 1960: 40). The phase dates from about A.D. 1000 to 1100 (Wasley 1959, Fig. 25) in a late Pueblo II stage of development.

During the Wingate Phase White Mountain Redware made its first appearance, and seems to have emerged from the indigenous black-on-white types. During this phase black-on-white remained the common color pattern. Puerco Black-on-white was apparently the most common type, but Red Mesa Black-on-white and Gallup Black-on-white were also present. White Mound Black-on-white, Kiatuthlanna Black-on-white, Red Mesa Black-on-white and Puerco Black-on-white exhibit a continuous sequential development through time in technology as well as in shape and design. During this development there appeared in the archaeological record the previously cited very small amounts of intrusive redware. Certain types such as Woodruff Red which has a red slip and Forestdale Black-on-red which does not have a red slip (Wendorf 1953: 115) may have been indigenous to the southwestern periphery of the Cibola area in the Petrified Forest, but in the present state of our knowledge they are too early to have materially affected the development of White Mountain Redware. The next redware to appear was that described by Roberts (1940: 50) as "early Developmental Pueblo black on red" and some sherds reported by Gladwin (1945: 57). Both authors suggested northern affinities for this ware. The sherds are possibly La Plata Black-on-red (Abel 1955), although Roberts reports sherd temper. Sherds are rare and associations uncertain, but "early Developmental Pueblo black on red" seems to belong in the Red Mesa Phase. This ware then probably sparked the development of Puerco Black-on-red and Wingate Black-on-red in the following Wingate Phase. Another type of slipped red pottery, which is a potential candidate for influencing the development of White Mountain Redware, is San Francisco Red of Mogollon derivation, but in view of its almost total absence in excavated sites in the Cibola area, and the fact that both Gladwin and Roberts imply northern affinities for the redware that is found earliest, the question of its influence cannot be answered. San Francisco Red is of considerable interest, however, as it disappeared (Wheat 1955) at about the time Puerco Black-on-red and Wingate Black-on-red began. More excavations on the southern edge of the Cibola area are needed.

All the attributes characteristic of the earliest White Mountain Redware, except the red slip, existed previously in the Cibola area before the advent of Puerco Black-on-red and Wingate Black-on-red. These attributes are light paste, black paint of either mineral or iron and carbon combinations, pitchers with long necks, bowls with flaring sides, sherd or sherd and sand or rock temper, the Puerco style of design, and the Dogoszhi style of design which seems to be ancestral to the Wingate style. The White Mountain Redware tradition began when these attributes first appeared in pottery with a red slip. It is possible that this emergence actually took place first in the Chaco, and the florescence of it in the Cibola area occurred only after the abandonment of the Chaco sometime in the early 1100's. The origin of the red slip is not clear. The slip is thick and not thin as on the northern black-on-reds and comes closer to that used on the local black-on-whites and on San Francisco Red. The paste of Puerco Black-on-red is more orange than that in later types. This may be a function of firing, of the clays used, or of the yellow limonite in the slip penetrating the paste to a greater extent than in later types. The major innovation in the development of redware was the substitution of yellow limonite—which is converted to a red ferric oxide when dehydrated by heating (Shepard 1956: 177)—for

whatever was used for a slip on the black-on-white pottery. If any changes in the firing method were required they were apparently effected. Pottery will fire white if the clays used are free from iron oxide, whether fired in an oxidizing or reducing atmosphere, providing there is no deposition of carbon (Shepard 1956: 221); and a clear-colored, fully oxidized paste may differ from an unoxidized gray one because of the time of firing rather than because it was subjected to a reducing atmosphere (Shepard 1956: 219).

The modal shapes in Puerco Black-on-red are the same as in Puerco Black-on-white. The most common shape in Puerco Black-on-red is a medium-sized bowl with rounded base and flaring sides. The most frequent jar shape is a pitcher with a long neck and a body with relatively high sharp or rounded shoulders. These same shapes seem to be the most common also in Puerco Black-on-white (Martin and Willis 1940, Pls. 70; 71, *3, 4, 7;* Olson and Wasley 1956, Fig. 242). This bowl shape was probably a continuation of the shape found in earlier black-on-white types which rarely had an incurved rim.

In Wingate Black-on-red, bowls with flaring sides and bowls with walls that become vertical just below the rim are equally common in occurrence. The latter form is not greatly different from the former and is probably a development from it. In Wingate Black-on-red, pitchers with long necks and sharp high shoulders occur, but the most common shape is one with medium shoulders and a neck intermediate in length between the long ones and the rather short ones typical of the type that followed, St. Johns Black-on-red.

In style, Puerco Black-on-red simply repeated the Holbrook and Puerco styles found on Puerco Black-on-white, although one bowl (Fig. 50) is closer to the earlier Red Mesa style. Wingate Black-on-red probably originated in Dogoszhi style (Fig. 51), and then rapidly developed its own Wingate style. The manner in which Wingate style differs from Dogoszhi style, as it is found on Gallup or Gallup-Chaco Black-on-white, is one of degree rather than of kind. Diagonal hatching is a distinctive attribute of both styles. In Dogoszhi style the hatching is usually broader than in Wingate style, but the ranges of the two styles overlap in this respect. Interlocked solid and hatched units are found in both styles and this highly significant development seems to have appeared first in Gallup Black-on-white, although uninterlocked hatched units by themselves are more common. Framing lines are

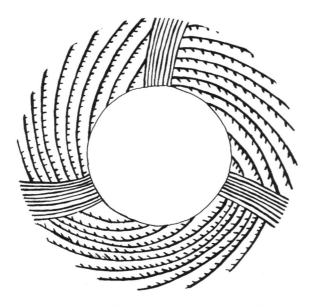

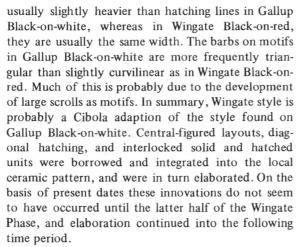

FIG. 50. Puerco Black-on-red bowl from Tusayan 16:3. The style is reminiscent of the earlier Red Mesa style.

FIG. 51. Wingate Black-on-red pitcher. The style is transitional between Dogoszhi and Wingate styles.

usually slightly heavier than hatching lines in Gallup Black-on-white, whereas in Wingate Black-on-red, they are usually the same width. The barbs on motifs in Gallup Black-on-white are more frequently triangular than slightly curvilinear as in Wingate Black-on-red. Much of this is probably due to the development of large scrolls as motifs. In summary, Wingate style is probably a Cibola adaption of the style found on Gallup Black-on-white. Central-figured layouts, diagonal hatching, and interlocked solid and hatched units were borrowed and integrated into the local ceramic pattern, and were in turn elaborated. On the basis of present dates these innovations do not seem to have occurred until the latter half of the Wingate Phase, and elaboration continued into the following time period.

Reserve Black-on-white differs in no way in modal style from Wingate Black-on-red, and it is probably also a Cibola pottery type although this needs additional documentation. It seems to have emerged from Puerco Black-on-white under the same stylistic influences which resulted in Wingate style on Wingate Black-on-red. Whether certain vessels are classified as Gallup Black-on-white or as Reserve Black-on-white seems to be partly a function of the area in which they are found rather than one of clear cut differences in the vessels themselves. Possibly a Gallup-Reserve Black-on-white should be defined which is

transitional in time, space, and style from Gallup Black-on-white to Reserve Black-on-white. Within such a category I would place those vessels from the Cibola area illustrated by Roberts (1932, Pls. 28 *f*, 30 *c*, 32 *f*, 33 *e*, 34 *c-d*, Figs. 19, 20; 1931, Pls. 14 *a-b*, 23 *c*, Fig. 29 *a*; 1940, Pl. 29 *a-b*). Reserve Black-on-white also employs the same bowl and jar shapes as Wingate Black-on-red. Typical examples of Reserve Black-on-white are illustrated by Martin and Willis (1940 Pls. 75-80) and by Martin and Rinaldo (1950 Figs. 192-3, 195-206).

The emergence of White Mountain Redware implemented one of the most significant trends in post-A.D. 1000 Anasazi ceramics, that is, the gradual domination and eventual absorption of most black-on-white pottery by the more brilliantly colored redwares. Within the Cibola area this trend started with the appearance of minor quantities of Puerco Black-on-red and Wingate Black-on-red during the Wingate Phase. I suspect Puerco Black-on-red was the more common of the two during this phase, but this cannot be documented satisfactorily. Once these types became reasonably common, which probably occurred in the latter part of this phase, they were traded to the west at least as far as Point of Pines (Breternitz 1959: 31), to the Pine Lawn Valley to the south (Martin and Rinaldo 1950: 501), and to the Chaco to the north, although the types may well have been made in the last-named area. Accompanying these two black-on-red types in their southern and western spread were probably Puerco Black-on-white and early forms of Reserve Black-on-white, as these types also appear in minor quantities in the Pine Lawn Valley (Martin and Rinaldo 1950, Fig. 216) and at Point of Pines (Breternitz 1959: 31-2).

EARLY PUEBLO III

The only major excavation in early Pueblo III sites in the Cibola area is that of Roberts (1932) at the Village of the Great Kivas. This site appears to occupy the time span of about A.D. 1100 to 1200. Judging from Roberts' illustrations the major black-on-white pottery type is Puerco Black-on-white (Roberts 1932, Pls. 24 c, 26 c, f, 29 c, 32 a-e, 33 a-d, 34 a-b, e, Figs. 23, 25, 26). However, a number of vessels best classified as Gallup-Reserve Black-on-white are present. Together with these types, Puerco Black-on-red, Wingate Black-on-red, and Wingate Polychrome seem to occur in quantity. The complex of painted pottery is largely that of the preceding Wingate Phase plus the two black-on-red types in greater quantity and the addition of Wingate Poly-chrome. The architectural stage is that of Pueblo III with large multi-room masonry structures.

The use of more than two colors on a vessel—which signifies a polychrome—is not strictly either a stylistic or a technolgical phenomenon, but in this case it apparently had its roots mainly in the technological aspects. Part of this lies in the ability of the potter to employ the proper ingredients in the construction of a vessel and to fire it so that the slip comes out red and the paste comes out light-colored or white. This had been accomplished during the preceding Wingate Phase. Wingate Polychrome marks the beginning of polychrome in the Cibola area, and was apparently the result of recognition by the potter of the potentialities of design inherent in a red slip covering a light paste. The earliest forms classifiable as polychrome are bowls and jars with a white circular area on the bottom which is not slipped. The color and design of these earliest vessels are typically either Wingate Black-on-red or Puerco Black-on-red and in sherd form most of them would probably be so classified. Experimentation with this color contrast probably led further to simple bands of light color and to placing crude duplications of the motifs used on bowl interiors on bowl exteriors. Additional experimentation may have led to the practice of using both white and red on bowl exteriors; either the red

could be applied first and the white afterward to cover the areas of the paste not covered by the slip, or the entire exterior could be covered with white slip paint on which red designs were placed. The former led to St. Johns Polychrome during late Pueblo III, which has a complete exterior red slip on bowls on which designs were placed in white paint, and the latter either became a dead end or continued later as a minor variant. White also began to appear on bowl interiors as an outline for black motifs in which case it was applied after the black paint. This may have been an outgrowth of the use of white paint on bowl exteriors.

The same sort of experimentation with designs in white slip paint on bowl exteriors was going on in Reserve Black-on-white. Finger dots, straight and curved broad lines, and other forms of crude decoration were sometimes applied over the unslipped paste on bowl exteriors (Martin and Rinaldo 1950: 503; Danson 1957: 92-3; Olson 1959: 105-7).

During early Pueblo III there seems to have been an increased use of polychrome at the expense of black-on-red pottery, and an increase in both at the expense of black-on-white. Bowls with walls that become vertical at the rim in both Puerco Black-on-red and Wingate Black-on-red probably belong to the early part of this time period, but were soon superseded by bowls with incurved rims. This inference is based on several facts and several other inferences: (1) Puerco Black-on-red seems to have declined as a type early in this period as the Puerco style of design appears much less commonly on Wingate Polychrome vessels; (2) bowls with flaring sides did not outlast this time period except as a bare percentage in St. Johns Polychrome; and (3) bowls with flaring sides seem developmentally related to bowls whose walls become vertical at the rim; these, in turn, are developmentally related to bowls whose walls incurve at the rim. Pitchers with long necks and high shoulders became less common during this period, and were replaced in part by pitchers with shorter necks and globular bodies. Strap handles on pitchers remained the mode, but lug handles appeared. This is probably to be correlated with the shortening of pitcher necks. Both unit and continuous patterns were placed on exteriors of polychrome bowls. Black-on-red bowls remained undecorated on the exterior except for small potters marks in black, with one exception (Fig. 8 m), on which a continuous pattern was applied, probably with the finger, in the slip paint before the bowl was fired. Tularosa style

FOUR MILE   STYLE

PINE-DALE   STYLE

TULAROSA   STYLE

PUERCO   STYLE

FIG. 52. Some sequent style changes.

developed late in this phase, probably not before A.D. 1175, as a result of the blending of Puerco style with Wingate style. This was coincident with a partial shift in slip color from red to orange-red.

Wingate Black-on-red, Puerco Black-on-red, and Wingate Polychrome were traded north to the Chaco and Mesa Verde, east to the other side of the Rio Grande, west as far as Wupatki, and south to what is now the Mexican border. As far as is known, they did not materially affect the ceramic patterns indigenous to these areas. Most trade was still to the north as far as the San Juan River.

LATE PUEBLO III

Late Pueblo III, from about A.D. 1200 to 1300, is known only from surface surveys and not from excavated sites in the Cibola area. The Gila Pueblo survey, however, strongly indicates this area as the center of distribution for St. Johns Polychrome and St. Johns Black-on-red. These probably became recognizable types by A.D. 1175 and overlapped with Wingate Black-on-red, Wingate Polychrome, and Puerco Black-on-red. Tularosa style itself seems to have been the result of a blending of Wingate style with Puerco style. From both these earlier styles came the preference for banded layouts. The central-figured layouts which are common in Wingate style are absent on vessels decorated in good Tularosa style. From Wingate style, Tularosa style obtained many of its motifs—scrolls, frets, double terrace units, and stepped squares—diagonal hatching, and the use of interlocked solid and hatched units with complicated edges. From Puerco style, Tularosa style obtained parallel hatching, vertically sectioned banded layouts, multiple concentric banded layouts, parallel-hatched panel dividers, and bands of parallel concentric hatching. Some influence from Mimbres style may have been responsible for the shift from Wingate to Tularosa style, particularly in regard to the shift from wide to narrower hatched units. Checkerboards and bands with negative units such as diamonds or parallelograms could have come from either Puerco or Mimbres style, although the former seems much more intimately related to Tularosa style in time and space.

Earlier design units were realigned in Tularosa style, so that it is distinct from both Wingate and Puerco styles. Much of the difference in appearance stems from the greater repetition of motifs made

possible by decreasing the size of the hatched units so that they are only slightly wider than their corresponding solid ones. Panel dividers began to be used in what would have been continuous patterns in Wingate style. Bands of concentric hatching were opposed by bands made up of solid, hatched, and negative units, whereas in Puerco style, the motifs would have been a band of parallel concentric hatching opposed by a solid band with negative units. New motifs appeared in the form of basketweave bands, reversed "Z" figures, vertical zigzags, and chains of joined parallelograms. These were actually largely recombinations of existing design units and were not markedly different from earlier motifs. The reversed "Z" figures, basketweave bands, and chains of joined parallelograms may be late, as they continued to be found on Pinedale Polychrome vessels which are decorated in Tularosa style.

Tularosa style, as it is found on Tularosa Black-on-white, seems to be the same in all modal attributes as in St. Johns Polychrome and St. Johns Black-on-red, and to have arisen from the styles of Puerco Black-on-white and Reserve Black-on-white. Tularosa Black-on-white occupied the time period of St. Johns Polychrome and has long been considered as belonging to the same culture as St. Johns Polychrome (Gladwin and Gladwin 1931: 38; Nesbitt 1938: 96; Reed 1955: 190). Puerco Black-on-white, Reserve Black-on-white, and Tularosa Black-on-white follow the same shape trends in pitchers (Martin and Rinaldo 1950: 503) as does the Puerco Black-on-red, Wingate Black-on-red, St. Johns Black-on-red sequence. Trends in bowl shapes are probably also identical. However, it is important to note that the number of bowls in the black-on-white types decreased through time, whereas the number of bowls per jar in the black-on-red types and St. Johns Polychrome increased materially through time. These trends are barely quantifiable. If the sample of redware in this study (which is not a random sample) were combined with St. Johns Black-on-red and St. Johns Polychrome in one temporal grouping, Wingate Black-on-red and Wingate Polychrome combined in a second temporal grouping, and Puerco Black-on-red in a third and earliest grouping, this trend is readily observable. The number of published illustrations of bowls and jars in Puerco Black-on-white are about equal, but Martin and Rinaldo (1950: 503), in a sample using sherds and whole vessels, report jars more common

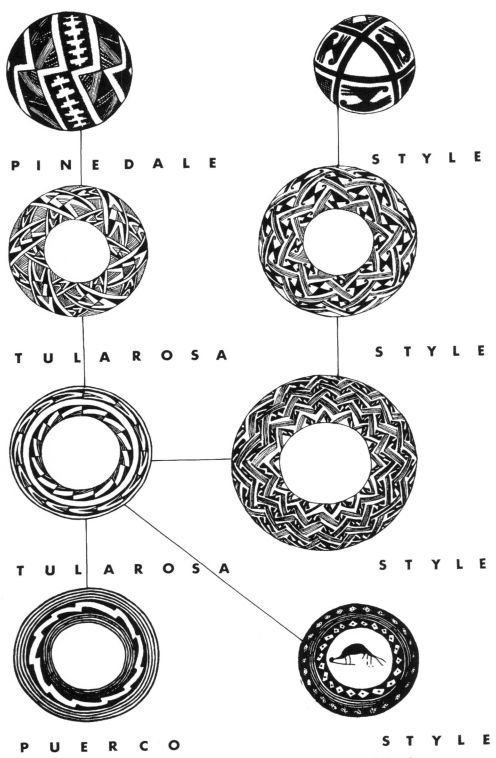

PINEDALE STYLE

TULAROSA STYLE

TULAROSA STYLE

PUERCO STYLE

FIG. 53. Some changes in and developments from multiple bands.

than bowls for Reserve Black-on-white. Colton and Hargrave (1937: 240) also report jars (pitchers) more common than bowls in Tularosa Black-on-white, and if the number of published illustrations of whole vessels of this type means anything, jars were far more common than bowls. None of these data are statistically reliable in the remotest sense, but are nevertheless indicative of a general trend toward the increase in black-on-red and polychrome bowls at the expense of black-on-white bowls. As a color scheme, black-on-white barely outlasted Pueblo III.

With the development of St. Johns Polychrome after A.D. 1175, the White Mountain Redware tradition expanded through trade and possibly through population movements to the south, southwest, and east. A few trade sherds have been found in the Chaco and as far north as Mesa Verde, but these are minimal. The large population centers in the Chaco had been abandoned by this time. There was a shift of population within the Cibola area away from the Puerco River valley slightly to the south and east. This inference is based on the slightly different center of distribution of St. Johns Polychrome compared with the preceding White Mountain Redware types.

The only effect the expansion of St. Johns Polychrome to the south into the Upper Gila area seems to have had on the indigenous pottery of the Mogollon is that its type of exterior white decoration was passed on to Reserve Plain and to Tularosa Fillet Rim to become Tularosa White-on-red (Nesbitt 1938: 98). The latter type occurs in increasing quantity during the Tularosa Phase in the Pine Lawn Valley (Martin, Rinaldo, and Barter 1957: Fig. 52). Rinaldo and Bluhm (1956: 154) suggest that the exterior white decoration on St. Johns Polychrome was derived from Tularosa White-on-red. I think this is unlikely.

To the east, St. Johns Polychrome was found in reasonable quantity at the Forked Lightning Ruin near Pecos (Kidder and Shepard 1936: 350) and both non-glaze and mat-glaze St. Johns Polychrome were present there. If St. Johns Polychrome had any effect on the indigenous pottery of the Rio Grande area, it remains to be defined. Glaze I Red (Kidder and Shepard 1936: Figs. 3, 4) developed on the stylistic level of Pinedale style, and is not decorated in Tularosa style.

To the southwest of the Cibola area, at Point of Pines, St. Johns Polychrome and St. Johns Black-on-red occur as tradeware together with Tularosa Black-on-white in the Tularosa Phase. The effect on the indigenous corrugated pottery seems to have been the development of McDonald Painted Corrugated and McDonald Patterned Corrugated from Reserve Indented Corrugated and Reserve Plain Corrugated. The first two types bear white painted motifs on the exteriors of vessels similar to those on St. Johns Polychrome, and appear in the Tularosa Phase (Breternitz, Gifford, and Olson, 1957, Fig. 2). Other types with white added to their textured decoration in an exuberance of varieties also began to be made.

In the area northeast of the Little Colorado, intermediate between the Hopi area on the north and the Cibola area on the east, St. Johns Polychrome seems to have affected the development of Klageto Polychrome and Kintiel Polychrome (Reed 1955: 183). These types have much the same color as St. Johns Polychrome and have either continuous or unit designs in white on the exteriors of bowls. The actual derivation of both types needs further study; the few examples I have seen look more like Hopi derivatives influenced by St. Johns Polychrome than derivatives of St. Johns Polychrome. Within the Hopi country itself, St. Johns Polychrome exterior designs also appear on Kwaituki Polychrome (Reed 1955: 183).

Along the upper Little Colorado River, long thought to be the center of distribution of St. Johns Polychrome (Gladwin and Gladwin 1931: 37), St. Johns Polychrome does not seem to be concentrated, but does occur in widely scattered sites ranging from small multi-room units to ruins with more than fifty rooms (Martin, Rinaldo, and Longacre 1961: 157). It is thought, on the basis of the present small sample of Springerville Polychrome centered in this area, that Springerville appeared here after A.D. 1250.

There were certain innovations which occurred during late Pueblo III and which reached their climax during the following period. Similarly, there were other trends which started late in the preceding phase and climaxed during this phase. The florescence of Tularosa style belongs to this period of about A.D. 1200 to 1275 although the style seems to have begun during the last decades preceding 1200. By 1200 Wingate Black-on-red, Puerco Black-on-red, and Wingate Polychrome disappeared as types and were succeeded by St. Johns Polychrome and St. Johns Black-on-red. The same may be said for Puerco Black-on-white and Reserve Black-on-white which seem to have developed into Tularosa Black-on-white by this time. Certain shape trends which affect all of these types have been referred to previously. The trend toward pitchers with shorter necks and lug handles climaxed during late Pueblo III, and by the end of this period this shape had almost disappeared. Bowls with incurved rims become the modal shape for bowls and this shape continued into following periods. Rims on bowls were frequently beveled inwardly with an external lip, whereas flattened and rounded self rims declined. Deep bowls are found during late Pueblo III, but are not common, and by its end bowls were all of medium depth.

There were several technological trends. The first was the shift in slip color from red to orange-red in St. Johns Polychrome and St. Johns Black-on-red. This shift was never adopted completely and red re-emerged as the modal color for Pinedale Polychrome and Pinedale Black-on-red. The cause of these shifts is unknown. Whether they were the result of different firing methods, of somewhat different constituents in the slip, possibly resulting from different sources of coloring matter available as a result of the population shifts, or simply of a change in style remain to be determined.

The surface treatment of vessels changed markedly in the shift from Wingate Polychrome to St. Johns Polychrome. In Wingate Black-on-red, Puerco Black-on-red, and Wingate Polychrome the exteriors of bowls usually have a rather rough appearance and exhibit rather broad polishing marks which do not leave the surface smooth. In Wingate Polychrome the different slip colors on bowl exteriors are run into one another during the polishing process and streaks of red appear on light areas and streaks of white on red areas. In St. Johns Polychrome bowl exteriors are much smoother in general. This is probably to be correlated with the fact that the exteriors of bowls were not used as a field of decoration in Wingate Black-on-red and Puerco Black-on-red and did not need to be particularly smooth. In Wingate Polychrome the method of applying exterior decoration on bowls militated against a smooth even appearance. In St. Johns Polychrome a reasonably smoothed exterior on bowls probably evolved hand in glove with the gradual use of this area as a field of decoration on which designs were painted in a contrasting color, as opposed to the earlier method in Wingate Polychrome when designs were formed from

the slip. The motor habits involved carried over into the smooth surfaces of St. Johns Black-on-red even though the white was not added to bowl exteriors.

The actual use of bowl exteriors as a field of decoration increased. This trend started during the preceding period with Wingate Polychrome and increased during all following periods. Several other trends became manifest, such as the general increase in polychrome over black-on-red, and the change in bowl form from previous shapes to bowls with incurved rims. The latter shape was probably a response to the use of bowl exteriors as a field of decoration. The upper exterior wall of bowls with incurved rims is much more open to view than this area on bowls with flaring sides or sides which rise vertically from slightly below the rim. All of these trends in style, shape, and technology are interrelated.

The motifs used on bowl exteriors were not markedly different from those used in the preceding Wingate Polychrome. They were narrower, but the same forms continued and became more varied (Fig. 54).

Motifs on jar necks changed from preceding modes. In Wingate Black-on-red and Puerco Black-on-red, motifs on jar necks are usually the same as on jar bodies. The different diameter of the two fields made for some variation in composition and interaction, but the units employed and the composition were basically the same. In St. Johns Black-on-red, however, this was no longer usual. Motifs on jar necks are almost invariably solid in composition rather than solid and hatched as on the jar bodies, and these motifs are the same as were used on St. Johns Polychrome bowl exteriors. The composition units on jar necks are black, whereas on bowl exteriors they are white.

Color patterns used for various fields shifted to some extent. White was used to outline motifs on bowl interiors to a limited extent throughout the period. This use started earlier, with Wingate Polychrome. During the time span of Wingate Polychrome and throughout most of that of St. Johns Polychrome, this outlining was applied after the black paint used for the primary motifs. Late in the time span of St. Johns Polychrome, there was experimentation in using black as well as white on bowl exteriors. Vessels which exhibit this feature are classified as Springerville Polychrome. This type appeared about A.D. 1250. Gradually this sequence—of first applying white and then black—probably began to be used on bowl interiors and on jars as well as on bowl exteriors. In very late St. Johns Polychrome and early Pinedale Polychrome in Tularosa style, both methods of application are present. In later types the white was invariably applied first.

The most striking technological development during late Pueblo III was the development of glaze. Judging from the technological studies that have been made, the preglaze black paint is for the most part a mixture of iron with some organic medium. Late St. Johns Polychrome and St. Johns Black-on-red were sometimes decorated with a black glaze paint of highly variable quality. Glazing was made possible, judging from the technological analyses (Kidder and Shepard 1936: 355, 362; Shepard 1942: 221-1; Haury and Hargrave 1931: 65), by the addition of copper, lead, and perhaps manganese in some form to the mixture of mineral and organic compounds already in use. Possibly kaolin was added also to give the paint its high silica content. Variations in firing may also have been partly responsible. Shepard (1942: 221) found insufficient lead in samples of Pinedale, Fourmile, and Heshota polychromes to affect the fusibility of the glaze, but all showed strong copper and silica content. Glazes gradually improved during Pueblo IV on the two Pinedale types and by the time of Cedar Creek, Fourmile, and Showlow polychromes, glaze was much better. The best glaze, per se, appears on some Heshota Polychrome vessels, although as an artistic medium it was less manageable than the more frequently mat-surfaced glaze of its Mogollon Rim contemporaries.

Pueblo III was ushered out by widespread population shifts in many areas of the Southwest. The most notable of these shifts were the abandonment of the Mesa Verde district about A.D. 1275-1300, with its population shifting at least in part to the Rio Grande, and the abandonment of portions of northern Arizona (Haury 1934: 149-55; 1958) for better watered areas to the south. These population movements caused a scrambling and mixing of the various regional cultural traditions of Pueblo III, and from this milieu emerged the traditions of Pueblo IV.

EARLY PUEBLO IV

By about A.D. 1300 St. Johns Polychrome and St. Johns Black-on-red had ceased to exist. Within the Cibola area itself Heshota Polychrome, Heshota Black-on-red, and Kwakina Polychrome had developed from St. Johns Polychrome and St. Johns Black-on-red, but never attained the geographic spread of the two earlier types. Atsinna was apparently founded about A.D. 1275-1300 as Woodbury and Woodbury (1966) report St. Johns Polychrome and Heshota Polychrome as the predominant pottery types with the latter gradually replacing the former. Reed (1955: 181) reports one of the various kinds of Klageto Black-on-white for the Zuni area. Cibola was no longer the only center for the manufacture of White Mountain Redware, however, as a second center with slightly divergent types had come into being along the Mogollon Rim, and possibly a third center in the Rio Grande area.

During and following the transition from Pueblo III to Pueblo IV, Pinedale Polychrome, Pinedale Black-on-red, and Pinedale Black-on-white became recognizable types in the Mogollon Rim area. Haury (Haury and Hargrave 1931) reports St. Johns Polychrome and Tularosa Black-on-white in the lower levels of the Showlow Ruin after A.D. 1200, and the Pinedale types were probably derived from them by 1275-1300, as they have been found at the Pinedale Ruin in contexts of this date. These early Pueblo IV types in the Mogollon Rim area are all decorated in Pinedale style. Many other pottery types of the same period are decorated in the same or closely related styles, for instance, Roosevelt Black-on-white, Jeddito Black-on-orange, Heshota Polychrome, Glaze I Red, Pinto Black-on-red, and Pinto Polychrome. It would appear that a plateau of stylistic development had been reached over a widespread area, and on this plateau Pinedale style elaborated rapidly on Cedar Creek Polychrome and evolved into Fourmile style.

Most of the influences which transformed Tularosa style into Pinedale style can be traced to the Kayenta-Hopi ceramic tradition to the north of the Mogollon Rim. The exact manner in which they were transferred is, however, somewhat of a problem. Part and parcel of this problem is the development of the Salado ceramic tradition which seems to center in the Tonto, Gila, and Roosevelt basins to the south and west of the Mogollon Rim, but whose pottery spread throughout the Southwest during Pueblo IV. The painted types which belong to this tradition are Pinto Black-on-red, Pinto Polychrome, Gila Black-on-red, Gila Polychrome, and Tonto Polychrome. The earliest

FIG. 54. Some changes and continuities in exterior decoration on bowls.

a. Point of Pines Polychrome   c. Cedar Creek Polychrome
b. Fourmile Polychrome.   d. Heshota Polychrome

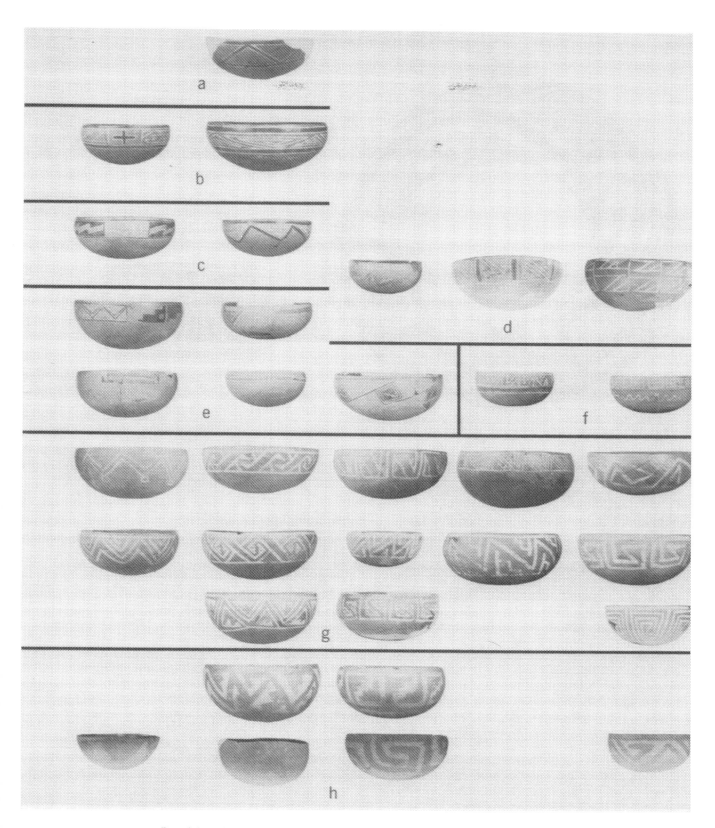

e. Pinedale Polychrome and Pinedale Black-on-red   *g.* St. Johns Polychrome

f. Springerville Polychrome   *h.* Wingate Polychrome

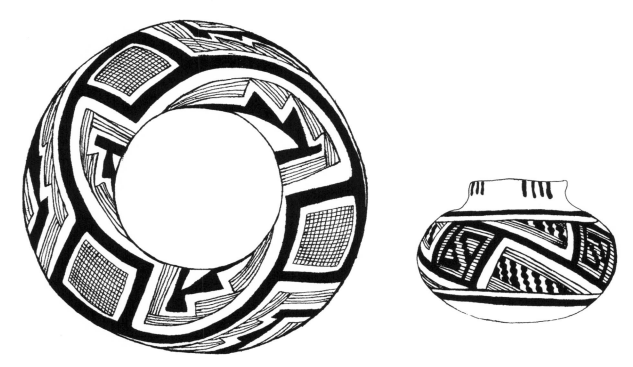

FIG. 55. Pinedale style. Squiggled or stepped line fillers. The "mosquito bar" technique, double banding
   lines, and the running diamond motif indicate relationships with the ceramics of northern Arizona.

of these types, Pinto Black-on-red and Pinto Polychrome, seem to have begun about the same time as
Pinedale Polychrome. The stylistic changes in the
Salado tradition are much the same as that in the
Pinedale-Cedar Creek-Fourmile development. Pinto
Polychrome and Pinto Black-on-red are occasionally
decorated in a style comparable to that on St. Johns
Polychrome, with closely massed units and sometimes
interlocked solid and hatched units. Later and more
common examples of this style are similar to Pinedale
style and comparable to that found on Cedar Creek
Polychrome. Gladwin and Gladwin (1930, Pl. 3 a-c)
illustrate some Cedar Creek Polychrome bowls, and
some Pinto Polychrome bowls (Pl. 4) which show the
strong stylistic relationships between the two types.
In the shift from Pinto Polychrome to Gila Polychrome, the major factor was the shift toward a
central focus of decoration on bowls. This is also the
stylistic shift which separates Cedar Creek Polychrome from Fourmile Polychrome. Other trends
common to the development of both Pinto-Gila and
Pinedale-Cedar Creek-Fourmile sequences are: (1)
the shift to broad bold patterns; (2) the shift away
from interlocked solid and hatched units; and (3) the
increasing use of parallel-hatched filler units and
squiggled line fillers. As far as can be ascertained,

these two ceramic developments were going through
these same shifts at approximately the same time, and
while they undoubtedly influenced one another,
neither of them appear to have originated the bold
decorative style, the central focus of decoration, or
the other primary developments in these stylistic
changes.
   Pinedale style first appears on a few vessels of late
St. Johns Polychrome. It is the modal style for
Pinedale Polychrome and Pinedale Black-on-red, and
probably for Pinedale Black-on-white. Cedar Creek
Polychrome is rarely decorated in any other style.
Those elements which are retained from Tularosa
style are: (1) the utilization of interlocked solid and
hatched units to form motifs; (2) the banded layout
and wall focus of decoration; (3) the curvilinear bird
figures; and (4) the preference for motifs in the form
of scrolls and frets. Those attributes which seem to
stem from the Kayenta-Hopi ceramic tradition
are: (1) the bold line work and bold patterns; (2)
filler units made up of small stepped lines; (3) filler
units of parallel hatching; (4) the running diamond
motif; (5) the offset quartered and negative offset
quartered layouts, and the whole idea of offsetting
layouts and design units; (6) double banding lines; (7)
the dotted edge used on many filler units; and (8) the

excellent artistry. Most of the above attributes are not reflected in Pinedale style as direct copies of Kayenta-Hopi ceramics, but were apparently reinterpreted and elaborated in Pinedale style. Elements such as bird figures (Figs. 52, 53) which were derived from Tularosa style were now larger and bolder, and so were all motifs. Offsetting was not used solely for offset quartered layouts, but for other layouts as well. Double banding lines very rarely exhibit line breaks as in the Kayenta-Hopi tradition. Double banding lines are not absent on vessels decorated in Tularosa style, but are considerably more frequent in vessels decorated in Pinedale style. One motif which was not borrowed is the "bat wing" scroll, the hallmark of the Salado.

The inference that these attributes were the result of influence from the Kayenta-Hopi ceramic tradition is based partly on the resemblances, and partly on the temporal priority of these attributes in the Kayenta-Hopi area. The bold style, the offset quartered layouts, the parallel-hatched filler units, and the stepped line filler units seem to have evolved gradually in that area from the time of Tusayan Polychrome (1150 - 1300), Kiet Siel Polychrome (1225 - 1300), Sagi Black-on-white (1200 - 1300), Jeddito Black-on-orange (1200 - 1300) and on into later types. Examples of these types are illustrated by Martin and Willis (1940). The Pinedale style of design which incorporated these attributes, and in turn elaborated them, did not appear until about 1275 - 1300. The temporal priority of these attributes in the Hopi-Kayenta tradition is not great, but does seem to involve a longer and more gradual sequence.

The development of Pinedale style is probably rooted in factors other than simple diffusion. The date A.D. 1275 marks the beginning of an intensive dry period which followed about a century of increasing aridity (Douglass 1929). The response to this intensive dry period seems to have been a movement of peoples to better watered areas where they could continue to practice agriculture. The cliff dwellings to the north of the Mogollon Rim in parts of the Kayenta-Hopi area were abandoned about this time (Haury 1934: 149-55), and that Kayenta peoples moved to the south has been more than amply demonstrated from the archaeological record at Point of Pines (Haury 1958). The style of decoration on the pottery made by these migrants to Point of Pines is very similar to Pinedale style. The time seems to have been one of cultural interchange between somewhat diverse peoples because of greater

proximity to one another. This interchange was probably responsible for the innovations and elaborations in Pinedale style which later resulted in Fourmile style, the techno-stylistic climax of the White Mountain Redware tradition.

Fourmile style differs from Pinedale style in only five significant aspects: (1) a center focus of decoration which is invariably found on Fourmile style bowls and is not found on Pinedale style bowls; (2) layouts which frequently lack bilateral symmetry; (3) framing lines which are always broader than hatching lines; (4) the absence of double banding lines; and (5) the rarity of interlocked solid and hatched units. The trend toward a center focus of decoration on bowls seems to have begun with a separate heavy banding line at the rim. Increasing the undecorated area between the separate banding line and the decoration itself eventually resulted in a center focus. Pinedale style seems to have borrowed double banding lines possibly from one of the Hopi types. Pinto Polychrome apparently did the same thing which transformed it into Gila Polychrome. In Jeddito Black-on-yellow (Martin and Willis 1940, Pls. 31-37), this trend developed even further with a wider area between the rim band and what had been its partner and thus a true central focus of decoration was developed. This trend occurs in other Kayenta-Hopi types (Bidahochi, Sikyatki, Chavez Pass, and Homolovi polychromes) also. In Fourmile Polychrome the line which had formerly been the heavy member of the double banding line at the rim of the bowl remained there, and the line which had formerly been the heavy member of the double banding line in the center of the bowl became the true framing line for the central focus of decoration. The Hopi-Kayenta types retained a comparatively narrow framing line for the central area of decoration, and so did Gila Polychrome.

Some shape changes occurred during early Pueblo IV. Pinedale Polychrome and Pinedale Black-on-red retained the basic shape of St. Johns Polychrome, a medium depth bowl with a rounded base and walls that incurve gently at the rim. Rim shapes changed somewhat. The most common rim shape in Pinedale Polychrome and Pinedale Black-on-red is rounded internally, but not beveled. This rim shape is not absent in St. Johns Polychrome, but the more common shape is internally beveled and frequently has an external lip. Jar shapes, too, changed during the time period of Pinedale Polychrome and Pinedale Black-on-red. If jars in these types are decorated in Tularosa

FOURMILE STYLE

PINEDALE STYLE

TULAROSA STYLE

WINGATE STYLE

PUERCO STYLE

FIG. 56. Some changes in and developments from frets.

style, and ·are therefore probably early, they are pitchers with short necks and lug handles. If they are decorated in Pinedale style, they are small or medium sized jars with short necks and no handles. This change may be interpreted as being either the culmination of the trend toward shorter necks and smaller handles, or as a disappearance of the pitcher and the incorporation of a new shape into the type. Specialized Kayenta-Hopi shapes, such as cups with small loop handles, do not appear in White Mountain Redware. In Cedar Creek Polychrome the same bowl shape with rounded base and gently incurved rim continued. Rims remained the same except that a few of them exhibit internal thickening. Jars became somewhat larger and usually have a white slipped area on the neck or shoulders or both. Jars with very short flaring necks appeared first in Cedar Creek Poly-chrome, but are more common in Fourmile Poly-chrome. Pinedale Black-on-white seems to have disappeared at about A.D. 1325 or slightly later at the time of the transition from Cedar Creek Poly-chrome to Fourmile Polychrome. The disappearance of this type is probably attributable to the increased preference for vessels with a polychrome color scheme. The shapes of Pinedale Black-on-white jars seem to have been incorporated into the color scheme of Fourmile Polychrome, leaving only the neck and shoulders white as a survival of their previous color. The neck ornamentation on the large jars of these two types is very similar (Haury and Hargrave 1931: 62).

Other shapes appeared in Fourmile Polychrome which were not previously present in White Mountain Redware. These are large jars with rather high shoulders and almost pointed bases (Fig. 37 *m*); jars with short flaring necks (Fig. 37 *e, k, l*) which in one instance, however, began in Cedar Creek Polychrome; "flower pot" shaped bowls (Fig. 37 *a-c*); parrot effigy vessels (Fig. 37 *h*); and small bowls with vertical sides and flattened bases (Fig. 36 *d*). Parrot and duck effigies are rather common in Roosevelt Black-on-white and the shape may have been incorporated from that type. "Flower pots" were possibly derived from the Salado culture. I have seen the shape in Tonto Polychrome. It also occurs in Showlow Glaze-on-white. The derivation of the small vertical sided bowls is uncertain. The large high shouldered jars seem more common in Gila Polychrome and were possibly derived from there. The jars with flaring necks may come from the same source or may

FIG. 57. Restored Cedar Creek Polychrome bowl. This is the most elaborate Pinedale style in the collection.

represent the incorporation of a plainware shape into the Fourmile color scheme.

Trends in exterior decoration change markedly during this period, and form the basis for the separation of some of the pottery types. A rather sudden shift to unit-type decoration on bowl exteriors occurred in Pinedale Polychrome and Pinedale Black-on-red; these unit designs are most characteristic of Pinedale Black-on-red, and of Pinedale Black-on-white. Similarly, Pinedale style is more characteristic of Pinedale Black-on-red than Pinedale Polychrome. Pinedale Black-on-red bowls are usually smaller than Pinedale Polychrome bowls. My feeling is that the direct transition from St. Johns Polychrome was to Pinedale Polychrome, and there was

more of a transition to Pinedale Black-on-red from Pinedale Black-on-white than from St. Johns Black-on-red to Pinedale Black-on-red. In Cedar Creek Polychrome the trend away from continuous patterns on bowl exteriors reversed itself, and continuous patterns again became more common. Black rim bands with pendant units probably appeared first, and later both upper and lower banding lines with narrow white line decoration between them became common. The latter are the mode in Cedar Creek Polychrome and remained the mode in Fourmile Polychrome and Showlow Polychrome, although rim bands with pendant units and black units between upper and lower banding lines were retained. The narrow white lines possibly developed from the idea of outlining a banding line or motif and then filling in the motif with black paint. By leaving off the black, white line patterns were produced. In Pinedale Polychrome some exterior motifs on bowls are white with elaboration in black placed over the white; these are in continuous patterns, and seem to represent the direct transition from the white continuous patterns of St. Johns Polychrome.

Fourmile style both developed and declined during early Pueblo IV. The style itself marks the techno-stylistic climax of the White Mountain Redware tradition with its radical departure from the rigid repetition of geometric units—derived mainly from textiles and characteristic of most earlier Anasazi styles—with its development of life forms (Figs. 49, 58) from these geometric motifs, and with its shift to a center focus of decoration on bowls, much more suitable to bowls with incurved rims than either a wall or whole field focus. Three other regional ceramic traditions in the Southwest preceded White Mountain Redware, however, in developing similar aspects of style. These traditions are the Hohokam, the Mimbres, and the Chihuahua, all non-Anasazi traditions. Life forms are found early in Hohokam types, but are quite different from the life forms in Fourmile style, and, indeed, seem to have disappeared from Hohokam types (Haury 1945: 55) long before the advent of Fourmile style. (No relationship is indicated.) Mimbres styles incorporated both life forms and a central focus of decoration on bowls and as such bear a stronger resemblance to Fourmile style. Mimbres style, however, also seems to have disappeared by A.D. 1200, long before the beginning of Fourmile style, and I see no relationship there either, unless remotely by way of the later Chihuahua polychromes or through some artistic medium other than pottery. The Chihuahua polychromes (Sayles 1936) apparently occupied the correct time period for influencing Fourmile style, but this influence seems to have been a causative factor in the obliteration of the White Mountain Redware tradition during late Pueblo IV rather than an inspiration for Fourmile style.

Even while the White Mountain Redware tradition was elaborating and reaching its climax between A.D. 1300 and 1400, the conditions for decline and eventual disappearance seem to have already been present. Part of the decline was probably the result of influence from other pottery traditions on the traditional color patterns of White Mountain Redware, black-on-red, and black-and-white-on-red, and part is

rooted in poorly-known factors which caused the abandonment of vast regions of the Southwest during Pueblo IV. There was a return to light colored (white, buff, yellow, cream) background colors on pottery, and a shift to the use of red paint for motifs rather than for a background color. Both of these traits appeared earlier outside the centers of redware manufacture in the polychromes of Chihuahua (Sayles 1936) and the influence causing these color shifts in White Mountain Redware possibly stemmed from that source.

A number of sites within the areas of manufacture of White Mountain Redware, occupied during early Pueblo IV, exhibit minor amounts of pottery closely related to White Mountain Redware, but which depart in color pattern. In the Mogollon Rim area, Showlow Polychrome, Kinishba Polychrome, Showlow Glaze-on-white, and local unnamed black-on-yellow types made their appearance (Cummings 1940; Haury and Hargrave 1931, Haury 1934; Baldwin 1938). In the Cibola area, Kwakina Polychrome, Kechipawan Polychrome (Hodge's Glaze D), Pinnawa Polychrome, Pinnawa Glaze-on-white (Hodge's Type C), Matsaki Brown-on-buff, and Matsaki Polychrome (Hodge's Glaze E) appeared at various times during Pueblo IV (Woodbury and Woodbury 1966). Some of the Rio Grande glazes (Kidder and Shepard 1936), beginning with Glaze I Yellow, exhibit much the same color shifts, but red seems never to have completely died out; it was used always, at least as a partial slip. These widespread changes are probably closely interrelated, as is the Hopi yellowware climax of late Pueblo IV and Pueblo V.

The conclusion adopted here is that this widespread change from redware to yellowware is at least partly the result of the florescence and disappearance of the cultures of northern Chihuahua where the ceramics typically exhibit a yellowish background color with red and black decoration (Sayles 1936). The tree-ring dates for Casas Grandes (Scott 1963) are not out of line with this hypothesis. One would suspect two routes of spread of these ceramic traits from Chihuahua: (1) northward up the Rio Grande valley, and (2) north and west through the San Pedro valley of southern Arizona to Cibola and the Mogollon Rim. I know of no good evidence for the first route. In regard to the second, Di Peso (1951: 124-9) has recognized a locally-made version of the Chihuahua polychromes, Babocomari Polychrome, in southeastern Arizona. This type may be one link in the

FIG. 58. Bird figures on Fourmile Polychrome bowls. The White Mountain Redware tradition is climaxed with the development of life forms from geometric units.

shift to yellowware—particularly to Kinishba Polychrome, Kechipawan Polychrome, Pinnawa Polychrome, and Matsaki Polychrome—in the northern
parts of the Southwest. A corollary of this hypothesis
is that many of the Mesoamerican traits attributed to
Pueblo III (Jennings 1956: 112) may not have
entered the Southwest until this period.

The viewpoint generally taken has been that local
yellowware found in the Mogollon Rim and Cibola
areas was the result of copying Jeddito Black-on-
yellow of the Hopi mesas, whereas the viewpoint
adopted here is that these peripheral yellowwares—
Kinishba Polychrome, Pinnawa Polychrome,
Kechipawan Polychrome, Matasaki Polychrome,
Matsaki Brown-on-buff, and other local black-on-
yellow types—originated under influence from
northern Mexico which spread northward, influenced
intervening pottery types first, and culminated in the
Hopi yellowware climax of late Pueblo IV and Pueblo
V. Burgh (1959) estimated the abrupt beginning of
yellowware at Awatovi at A.D. 1300; but, on the
above theoretical basis A.D. 1350 to 1400 would
seem more likely. These slightly later dates are not
without some basis in fact. At the Showlow Ruin,
Jeddito Black-on-yellow was almost unknown as late
as A.D. 1383 (Haury and Hargrave 1931: 44), with a
single sherd of this type found with a timber dated
about 1375, although Matsaki Polychrome (Hodge's
Glaze E), Kechipawan Polychrome (Hodge's Glaze
D), and local black-on-yellow were present. In the
Sierra Ancha (Haury 1934), the situation is similar,
for both Kinishba Polychrome (black-and-red-on-
yellow) and local black-on-yellow are reported
together with Fourmile Polychrome in contexts dated
A.D. 1326 to 1348. At Kinishba (Cummings 1940),
Kinishba Polychrome, a vessel tentatively identified
by the Woodburys (1966) as Kechipawan Polychrome, and black-on-yellow, which could be of local
manufacture, were found. Fourmile Polychrome was
found in quantity at all these sites. These data suggest
that the transition from red to yellowware was in
progress at the time of the abandonment of these
sites in the late fourteenth century, and give no clear
indication that Jeddito Black-on-yellow had developed prior to A.D. 1375. On the basis of strict
typological comparisons it is nearly impossible to
differentiate internal developments from external
influences in these color changes starting in early
Pueblo IV. There was certainly continuity from
earlier types, and there was certainly a shift in
background color from orange or red to yellow or

buff which was neither difficult to achieve nor
lacking in the potentialities of the earlier redware.
But the question still arises, why did the shift occur?
Many more comparisons need to be made.

LATE PUEBLO IV

Late Pueblo IV, from about A.D. 1400 to the time
of the arrival of the Spaniards in 1540, is one of the
least understood and most complicated periods in
Southwestern prehistory. Cultural decline is evident
in almost all areas of the Southwest in 1540, except
on the Hopi mesas, in the "Seven Cities of Cibola,"
and in the Rio Grande region. Only in these areas still
occupied by pueblo peoples was decline not evident.
Hohokam culture had climaxed and degenerated. The
centers of high culture in Chihuahua had disappeared
by this period. The Mogollon Rim had been abandoned and the areas between the Mogollon Rim and
the Hopi mesas and between the Mogollon Rim and
Cibola were probably in the process of being abandoned. There survived in the White Mountains of
Arizona, until approximately 1450, a small group
which made Point of Pines Polychrome, a degenerate
version of Fourmile Polychrome. One historic group,
the Tsipiakwe, may have survived in the area between
Hopi and Zuni until as late as 1632, but there is
considerable confusion as to whether they were
located there or to the south on the Salt River
(Hodge 1912: 827).

By late Pueblo IV yellowware had all but eclipsed
the earlier redware in almost every area of the
Southwest. Partial red slips survived on the Rio Grande
glazes and were in turn reintroduced into the Cibola
area at about 1630 on Hawikuh Polychrome (Woodbury and Woodbury 1966). The indigenous pottery
types in the Cibola area at this time were Matsaki
Polychrome and Matsaki Brown-on-buff, types which
apparently stemmed from Kechipawan Polychrome
during the fifteenth century (Woodbury and Woodbury 1966).

While the Zuni enter history in the Cibola area as
the probable descendants of the earlier manufacturers
of many types of White Mountain Redware, the
people who inhabited the Mogollon Rim and made
similar types of the same ware disappeared from the
archaeological record at about A.D. 1400. While the
identity of their descendants, if there are any, will
possibly remain in doubt forever, the traditional
histories of both Hopi and Zuni mention movements
of people from the region south of the Hopi mesas

FIG. 59. Late White Mountain Redware bowls with flower designs. Left: Point of Pines Polychrome. Right: crude Fourmile Polychrome bowl from the Banning Wash Ruin. Flowers as well as other motifs suggest relationships between Fourmile and Sikyatki styles.

and west of Zuni. The pueblos of Homolobi near Winslow, Arizona, figure prominently in Hopi legend and are indeed the only known pueblos—where Fourmile Polychrome is commonly found—which do have traditions concerning them. It is tempting to correlate the makers of Fourmile Polychrome with the "Sun people" who came from the "Red Land" in the south, built a village with the "Water people" at Homolobi, and later moved to Awatovi and the Middle Mesa (Mindeleff 1891: 29). Sikyatki Polychrome of the Hopi mesas does bear a generalized similarity to Fourmile Polychrome in style; its asymmetry, use of life forms, flowers (Fig. 59), F-hooks, bird-shaped frets, and other features do suggest a relationship. Sikyatki style seems to complete the trend toward life forms which started in Fourmile style and culminated with near realism in Sikyatki style. Smith (1952: 148) sees the designs of Fourmile, Homolobi, and Showlow polychromes as the impetus which started the "Jeddito school of design" on its flamboyant way. Zuni legends (Cushing 1896) indicate that the historic group was formed from two segments, an early group coming from the north and a later one from the west or southwest. While the distributions of White Mountain Redware types during Pueblo II are suggestive of an origin slightly to

the north of historic Zuni country, and the extension of White Mountain Redware to the Mogollon Rim during very late Pueblo III suggests a movement from the Cibola area, and consequently the possibility of a return during later times of stress, there is little to indicate that any such return was ever made. A detailed comparison of Fourmile style with that of Matsaki Polychrome, on the one hand, and with Sikyatki Polychrome, on the other, might help to answer this question. Fourmile style is possibly ancestral to both. One attribute which does suggest relationships of Fourmile Polychrome with Matsaki Polychrome is outlining. On all the Hopi types of this period the outlining on motifs was put on after the motif had been painted, whereas on Fourmile Polychrome and on the one actual example of Matsaki Polychrome that I have seen, the outlining was applied first and the design was then filled in. More data are needed to carry these inferences further, but it seems quite possible that people who occupied the Mogollon Rim during Pueblo IV migrated to both Hopi and Zuni areas during the late fourteenth and early fifteenth centuries. This would also be the time of transition from red to yellowware. More work needs to be done in the late ruins in the area between the Mogollon Rim and the Hopi mesas and Zuni.

5. SUMMARY AND CONCLUSIONS

At about A.D. 1000 the White Mountain Redware tradition originated within the Cibola area of west-central New Mexico with the appearance first of Puerco Black-on-red, and, slightly later, of Wingate Black-on-red. These events occurred during the Wingate Phase. The shapes and styles of these types were derived from the indigenous black-on-white pottery of this area. There are several possible sources for the idea of slipping pottery red. Holbrook, Puerco, and Wingate styles were in use.

During the following period, early Pueblo III, from about A.D. 1100 - 1200, Wingate style became more popular and was elaborated. Reserve Black-on-white developed as the white-slipped counterpart of Wingate Black-on-red. Wingate Polychrome began early in this period as a derivative of Puerco Black-on-red and Wingate Black-on-red. Later in this period, after about A.D. 1175, St. Johns Polychrome and St. Johns Black-on-red decorated in Tularosa style emerged as a development from the preceding types. Tularosa is the result of a gradual blending of Wingate and Puerco styles. Tularosa Black-on-white belongs to the same style and time period and probably to the same culture. Related shape trends are found in all these types.

During late Pueblo III, from about A.D. 1200 to 1275, St. Johns Polychrome and St. Johns Black-on-red spread by trade to the east, south, southeast, and west and influenced ceramic developments in the upper Gila, White Mountains, Little Colorado, and Mogollon Rim areas. Polychrome became the most popular color scheme particularly for large bowls, whereas black-on-white remained the colors most used for jar and small bowl shapes. Between A.D. 1275 and 1300 there was a churning and moving of populations in the Southwest, possibly as the result of a prolonged drought. Before the close of this period Pinedale Polychrome and Pinedale Black-on-red became established in the Mogollon Rim area, and Heshota Polychrome, Heshota Black-on-red, and Kwakina Polychrome developed in the Cibola area. White Mountain Redware had diverged into two regional variants which are derivatives of St. Johns Polychrome. There is probably a third regional development in the Rio Grande valley.

During Pueblo IV, from about A.D. 1300 to 1400, the pottery types within these areas continued to develop, but were eventually replaced by pottery with other color schemes. In the Cibola area Heshota Polychrome, Heshota Black-on-red, and Kwakina Polychrome gradually disappeared as types and changed into Kechipawan Polychrome, Pinnawa Glaze-on-white, and Pinnawa Red-on-white which were followed about 1500 by Matsaki Brown-on-buff and Matsaki Polychrome. These types are no longer redware and the White Mountain Redware tradition was eclipsed in this area. In the Mogollon Rim area stylistic change was rapid and Pinedale style developed on Pinedale Polychrome, Pinedale Black-on-red, Pinedale Black-on-white, and Cedar Creek Polychrome. Pinedale style evolved as an elaboration of what was basically Tularosa style through the incorporation of traits originating in the Kayenta-Hopi ceramic tradition. These influences could have come either by way of the Salado ceramic tradition, which goes through much the same stylistic change, or directly from the Kayenta-Hopi ceramic tradition. Fourmile style grew out of Pinedale style largely as a result of its emphasis on a central focus of decoration on bowl interiors. The central focus of decoration is a stylistic arrangement which builds up gradually in the Kayenta-Hopi pottery tradition and Fourmile style probably obtained it from that source. The technostylistic development of the White Mountain Redware tradition climaxed in Fourmile Polychrome.

White Mountain Redware was eventually submerged by yellowware. This preference for pottery with a yellow or buff background was widespread during Pueblo IV and may have originated in Chihuahua. White Mountain Redware was affected by it before the last redware had disappeared, and Kinishba Polychrome, Kechipawan Polychrome, and other black-on-yellow pottery began to be manufactured. Before this trend culminated the Mogollon Rim area was abandoned. Degenerate versions of Fourmile Polychrome and Point of Pines Polychrome lived on for about another 50 years at Point of Pines, and then this area was deserted also. Stylistic relationships exist between Fourmile Polychrome, Matsaki Polychrome, and Sikyatki Polychrome which suggest that the descendants of the manufacturers of White Mountain Redware are to be found among the historic Hopi and Zuni.

REFERENCES

ABEL, L. J.
  1955   Pottery Types of the Southwest: Wares 5A, 10A, 10B, 12A, San Juan Red Ware, Mesa Verde Gray, and White Ware, San Juan White Ware. *Museum of Northern Arizona, Ceramic Series*, No. 3B. Flagstaff.

AMSDEN, C. A.
  1936   An Analysis of Hohokam Pottery Design. *Medallion Papers,* No. 23. Gila Pueblo, Globe.

BALDWIN, G. C.
  1938   A New Pottery Type from Eastern Arizona. *Southwestern Lore*, Vol. 4, No. 2, 21-6. Gunnison.

BARTER, E. R.
  1955   An Analysis of the Ceramic Traditions of the Jewett Gap Site, New Mexico. MS, master's thesis, University of Arizona, Tucson.

BRETERNITZ, D. A.
  1959   Excavations at Nantack Village, Point of Pines, Arizona. *Anthropological Papers of the University of Arizona,* No. 1. Tucson.

BRETERNITZ, D. A., JAMES C. GIFFORD, AND ALAN P. OLSON
  1957   Point of Pines Phase Sequence and Utility Pottery Type Revisions. *American Antiquity,* Vol. 22, No. 4, pp. 412-16. Salt Lake City.

BURGH, ROBERT F.
  1959   Ceramic Profiles in the Western Mound at Awatovi, Northeastern Arizona. *American Antiquity,* Vol. 25, No. 2, pp. 184-202. Salt Lake City.

CASSIDY, F. E.
  1956   Excavated Sites: LA 2520. In *Pipeline Archaeology,* edited by Fred Wendorf, Nancy Fox, and O. L. Lewis, pp. 16-21. Laboratory of Anthropology and Museum of Northern Arizona, Santa Fe and Flagstaff.

CHAPMAN, K. M., AND B. T. ELLIS
  1951   The Line-Break, Problem Child of Pueblo Pottery. *El Palacio,* Vol. 58, No. 9, pp. 251-89. Santa Fe.

CLARKE, E. P.
  1935   Designs on the Prehistoric Pottery of Arizona. *University of Arizona Bulletin,* Vol. 6, No. 4, *Social Science Bulletin,* No. 9, Tucson.

COLTON, H. S.
  1953   Potsherds: An Introduction to the Study of Prehistoric Southwestern Ceramics and Their Use in Historic Reconstruction. *Museum of Northern Arizona, Bulletin* 25. Flagstaff.
  1955   Check List of Southwestern Pottery Types. *Museum of Northern Arizona, Ceramic Series,* No. 2. Flagstaff.

COLTON, H. S., AND L. L. HARGRAVE
  1937   Handbook of Northern Arizona Pottery Wares. *Museum of Northern Arizona, Bulletin* 11. Flagstaff.

COSGROVE, H. S., AND C. B. COSGROVE
  1932   The Swarts Ruin: A Typical Mimbres Site in Southwestern New Mexico. *Papers of the Peabody Museum, Harvard University,* Vol. 15, No. 1. Cambridge.

CUMMINGS, BYRON
  1940   *Kinishba: A Prehistoric Pueblo of the Great Pueblo Period.* Hohokam Museums Association and the University of Arizona, Tucson.

CUSHING, F. H.
  1896   Outlines of Zuñi Creation Myths. *Thirteenth Annual Report of the Bureau of Ethnology,* pp. 321-447. Washington.

DANSON, E. B.
  1957   An Archaeological Survey of West Central New Mexico and East Central Arizona. *Papers of the Peabody Museum, Harvard University,* Vol. 44, No. 1. Cambridge.

DIPESO, C. C.

1951   The Babocomari Village Site on the Babocomari River, Southeastern Arizona. *The Amerind Foundation*, No. 5. Dragoon.

DITTERT, A. E., JR.

1959   Culture Change in the Ceballeta Mesa Region, Central Western New Mexico. MS, doctoral dissertation, University of Arizona, Tucson.

DOUGLASS, A. E.

1929   The Secret of the Southwest Solved by Talkative Tree Rings. *National Geographic Magazine*, Vol. 56, No. 6, pp. 737-70. Washington.

1938   Southwestern Dated Ruins: V. *Tree-Ring Bulletin*, Vol. 5, No. 2, pp. 10-13. Flagstaff.

DUTTON, B. P.

1939   Leyit Kin, A Small House Ruin, Chaco Canyon, New Mexico: Excavation Report. *Monographs of the School of American Research*, No. 7. Santa Fe.

FEWKES, J. W.

1904   Two Summers' Work in Pueblo Ruins. *22nd Annual Report of the Bureau of American Ethnology*, Part 1, pp. 3-195. Washington. .

GIFFORD, J. C.

1957   Archaeological Explorations in Caves of the Point of Pines Region. MS, master's thesis, University of Arizona, Tucson.

GIFFORD, J. C. (EDITOR)

1953   *A Guide to the Description of Pottery Types in the Southwest.* Prepared by the Archaeological Seminar of the Department of Anthropology at the University of Arizona, Spring, 1952. Tucson.

GLADWIN, H. S.

1945   The Chaco Branch: Excavations at White Mound and in the Red Mesa Valley. *Medallion Papers*, No. 33. Gila Pueblo, Globe.

GLADWIN, WINIFRED, AND H. S. GLADWIN

1930   Some Southwestern Pottery Types: Series I. *Medallion Papers*, No. 8. Gila Pueblo, Globe.

1931   Some Southwestern Pottery Types: Series II. *Medallion Papers*, No. 10. Gila Pueblo, Globe.

1934   A Method for Designation of Cultures and Their Variations. *Medallion Papers*, No. 15. Gila Pueblo, Globe.

HARGRAVE, L. L.

1929   Elden Pueblo. *Museum of Northern Arizona, Museum Notes*, Vol. 2, No. 5. Flagstaff.

1932   Guide to Forty Pottery Types from the Hopi Country and the San Francisco Mountains, Arizona. *Museum of Northern Arizona, Bulletin* 1. Flagstaff.

HAURY, E. W.

1930   A Sequence of Decorated Redware from the Silver Creek Drainage. *Museum of Northern Arizona, Museum Notes*, Vol. 2, No. 11, p. 4. Flagstaff.

1932   The Age of Lead Glaze Decorated Pottery in the Southwest. *American Anthropologist*, n.s., Vol. 34, pp. 418-25. Menasha.

1934   The Canyon Creek Ruin and the Cliff Dwellings of the Sierra Ancha. *Medallion Papers*, No. 14. Gila Pueblo, Globe.

1945   The Excavation of Los Muertos and Neighboring Ruins in the Salt River Valley, Southern Arizona. *Papers of the Peabody Museum, Harvard University*, Vol. 24, No. 1. Cambridge.

1958   Evidence at Point of Pines for a Prehistoric Migration from Northern Arizona. In "Migrations in New World Culture History," edited by R.H. Thompson, pp. 1-6. *University of Arizona Bulletin*, Vol. 29, No. 2, *Social Science Bulletin*, No. 27. Tucson.

HAURY, E. W. AND L. L. HARGRAVE
  1931   Showlow and Pinedale Ruins. In "Recently Dated Pueblo Ruins in Arizona," *Smithsonian Miscellaneous Collections,* Vol. 82, No. 11, pp. 4-79. No. 11, Washington.

HAWLEY, F. M.
  1929   Prehistoric Pottery Pigments of the Southwest. *American Anthropologist,* n.s., Vol. 31, No. 4, pp. 731-54. Menasha.
  1934   The Significance of the Dated Prehistory of Chetro Ketl, Chaco Cañon, New Mexico. *Monographs of the School of American Research,* No. 2. Santa Fe.
  1950   Field Manual of Prehistoric Southwestern Pottery Types, revised edition. *University of New Mexico Bulletin, Anthropological Series,* Vol. 1, No. 4. Albuquerque.

HODGE, F. W. (EDITOR)
  1912   Handbook of American Indians North of Mexico. *Bureau of American Ethnology, Bulletin* 30. Washington.

HOUGH, WALTER
  1903   Archeological Field Work in Northeastern Arizona. The Museum-Gates Expedition of 1901. *Annual Report of the United States National Museum for 1901,* pp. 279-358. Washington.
  1930   Exploration of Ruins in the White Mountain Apache Indian Reservation, Arizona. *Proceedings of the United States National Museum,* 1-21. Washington.

JENNINGS, J. D. (EDITOR)
  1956   The American Southwest: A Problem in Cultural Isolation. In "Seminars in Archaeology: 1955," edited by Robert Wauchope, pp. 59-127. *Memoirs of the Society for American Archaeology,* No. 11. Salt Lake City.

JUDD, N. M.
  1954   The Material Culture of Pueblo Bonito. *Smithsonian Miscellaneous Collections,* Vol. 124, Washington.
  1959   Pueblo del Arroyo, Chaco Canyon, New Mexico. *Smithsonian Miscellaneous Collections,* Vol. 138, No. 1. Washington.

KIDDER, A. V. AND A. C. SHEPARD
  1936   The Pottery of Pecos, Vol. 2. *Papers of the Phillips Academy, Southwestern Expedition,* No. 7. Yale University Press, New Haven.

MARTIN, P. S. AND J. B. RINALDO
  1950   Sites of the Reserve Phase, Pine Lawn Valley, Western New Mexico. *Fieldiana: Anthropology,* Vol. 38, No. 3. Chicago Natural History Museum, Chicago.
  1960   Excavations in the Upper Little Colorado Drainage, Eastern Arizona. *Fieldiana: Anthropology,* Vol. 51, No. 1. Chicago Natural History Museum, Chicago.

MARTIN, P. S., J. B. RINALDO, AND E. R. BARTER
  1957   Late Mogollon Communities: Four Sites of the Tularosa Phase, Western New Mexico. *Fieldiana: Anthropology,* Vol. 49, No. 1. Chicago Natural History Museum, Chicago.

MARTIN, P. S., J. B. RINALDO, AND E. A. BLUHM
  1954   Caves of the Reserve Area. *Fieldiana: Anthropology,* Vol. 42, Chicago Natural History Museum, Chicago.

MARTIN, P. S., J. B. RINALDO, E. A. BLUHM, AND H.C. CUTLER
  1956   Higgins Flat Pueblo, Western New Mexico. *Fieldiana: Anthropology,* Vol. 45. Chicago Natural History Museum, Chicago.

MARTIN, P. S., J. B. RINALDO, E. A. BLUHM, H. C. CUTLER, AND R. T. GRANGE, JR.
  1952   Mogollon Cultural Continuity and Change: The Stratigraphic Analysis of Tularosa and Cordova Caves. *Fieldiana: Anthropology,* Vol. 40. Chicago Natural History Museum, Chicago.

MARTIN, P. S., J. B. RINALDO, AND W. A. LONGACRE
1961   Mineral Creek Site and Hooper Ranch Pueblo, Eastern Arizona. *Fieldiana: Anthropology,* Vol. 52, Chicago Natural History Museum, Chicago.

MARTIN, P. S. AND E. S. WILLIS
1940   Anasazi Painted Pottery in the Field Museum of Natural History. *Field Museum of Natural History, Anthropology Memoirs,* Vol. 5. Chicago.

MERA, H. P.
1934   Observations on the Archaeology of the Petrified Forest National Monument. *Laboratory of Anthropology, Technical Series Bulletin* No. 7. Santa Fe.
1935   Ceramic Clues to the Prehistory of North Central New Mexico. *Laboratory of Anthropology, Technical Series Bulletin,* No. 8. Santa Fe.
1939   Style Trends of Pueblo Pottery in the Rio Grande and Little Colorado Cultural Areas from the Sixteenth to the Nineteenth Century. *Memoirs of the Laboratory of Anthropology,* Vol. 3. Santa Fe.

MINDELEFF, VICTOR
1891   A Study of Pueblo Architecture: Tusayan and Cibola. *Eighth Annual Report of the Bureau of Ethnology,* pp. 3-228. Washington.

MORRIS, E. A.
1957   Stratigraphic Evidence for a Cultural Continuum at the Point of Pines Ruin. MS, master's thesis, University of Arizona, Tucson.

MORRIS, E. H.
1939   Archaeological Studies in the La Plata District, Southwestern Colorado and Northwestern New Mexico. *Carnegie Institution of Washington, Publication* 519. Washington.

NESBITT, P. H.
1938   Starkweather Ruin: A Mogollon-Pueblo Site in the Upper Gila Area of New Mexico, and Affiliative Aspects of the Mogollon Culture. *Logan Museum Publications in Anthropology, Bulletin* No. 6. Beloit.

OLSON, A. P.
1959   An Evaluation of the Phase Concept in Southwestern Archaeology: As Applied to the Eleventh and Twelfth Century Occupations at Point of Pines, East Central Arizona. Doctoral dissertation, University of Arizona. University Microfilms, Ann Arbor.

OLSON, A. P., AND W. W. WASLEY
1956   An Archaeological Traverse Survey in West-Central New Mexico. In *Pipeline Archaeology,* edited by Fred Wendorf, Nancy Fox, and O. L. Lewis, pp. 256-390. Laboratory of Anthropology and Museum of Northern Arizona, Santa Fe and Flagstaff.

PHILLIPS, PHILIP
1958   Application of the Wheat-Gifford-Wasley Taxonomy to Eastern Ceramics. *American Antiquity,* Vol. 24, No. 2, pp. 117-25. Salt Lake City.

RANDS, R. L.
1961   Elaboration and Invention in Ceramic Traditions. *American Antiquity,* Vol. 26, No. 3, pp. 331-40. Salt Lake City.

REED, E. K.
1955   Painted Pottery and Zuñi History. *Southwestern Journal of Anthropology,* Vol. 11, No. 5, pp. 178-93. Albuquerque.

RINALDO, J. B.
1959   Foote Canyon Pueblo, Eastern Arizona. *Fieldiana: Anthropology,* Vol. 49, No. 2. Chicago Natural History Museum, Chicago.
1961   Mineral Creek Site and Hooper Ranch Pueblo, Eastern Arizona. *Fieldiana: Anthropology,* Vol. 52. Chicago Natural History Museum, Chicago.

RINALDO, J. B. AND E. A. BLUHM
1956   Late Mogollon Pottery Types of the Reserve Area. *Fieldiana: Anthropology,* Vol. 36, No. 7, pp. 149-187. Chicago Natural History Museum, Chicago.

ROBERTS, F. H. H., JR.
1931   The Ruins at Kiatuthlanna, Eastern Arizona. *Bureau of American Ethnology, Bulletin* 100. Washington.

1932   The Village of the Great Kivas on the Zuñi Reservation, New Mexico. *Bureau of American Ethnology, Bulletin* 111. Washington.

1939   Archeological Remains in the Whitewater District, Eastern Arizona: Part I. House Types. *Bureau of American Ethnology, Bulletin* 121. Washington.

1940   Archeological Remains in the Whitewater District, Eastern Arizona: Part II. Artifacts and Burials. *Bureau of American Ethnology, Bulletin* 126. Washington.

SAYLES, E. B.
1936   Some Southwestern Pottery Types, Series V. *Medallion Papers,* No. 21. Gila Pueblo, Globe.

SCHMIDT, E. F.
1928   Time-Relations of Prehistoric Pottery Types in Southern Arizona. *Anthropological Papers of the American Museum of Natural History,* Vol. 30, Part 5, pp. 247-302. New York.

SCOTT, S. D.
1963   Tree-Ring Dating in Mexico. MS, doctoral dissertation, University of Arizona, Tucson.

SECOND SOUTHWESTERN CERAMIC SEMINAR
1959   Museum of Northern Arizona. Flagstaff.

SHEPARD, A. O.
1942   Rio Grande Glaze Paint Ware: A Study Illustrating the Place of Ceramic Technological Analysis in Archaeological Research. *Carnegie Institution of Washington, Publication* 528, pp. 129-260. Washington.

1956   Ceramics for the Archaeologist. *Carnegie Institution of Washington, Publication* 609. Washington.

SMILEY, T. L.
1951   A Summary of Tree-Ring Dates from Some Southwestern Archaeological Sites. *University of Arizona Bulletin,* Vol. 22, No. 4, *Laboratory Bulletin of Tree-Ring Research,* No. 5. Tucson.

1952   Four Late Prehistoric Kivas at Point of Pines, Arizona. *University of Arizona Bulletin,* Vol. 23, No. 3, *Social Science Bulletin,* No. 21. Tucson.

SMILEY, T.L., S.A. STUBBS, AND BRYANT BANNISTER
1953   A Foundation for the Dating of Some Late Archaeological Sites in the Rio Grande Area, New Mexico: Based on Studies in Tree-Ring Methods and Pottery Analyses. *University of Arizona Bulletin,* Vol. 24, No. 3, *Laboratory of Tree-Ring Research Bulletin,* No. 6. Tucson.

SMITH, WATSON
1952   Kiva Mural Decorations at Awatovi and Kawaika-a with a Survey of Other Wall Paintings in the Pueblo Southwest. *Papers of the Peabody Museum, Harvard University,* Vol. 37. Cambridge.

SMITH, WATSON, RICHARD B. WOODBURY, AND NATHALIE F. S. WOODBURY
1966   The Excavation of Hawikuh by Frederick Webb Hodge. *Contributions from the Museum of the American Indian, Heye Foundation,* Vol. XX. New York.

SPIER, LESLIE
1917   An Outline for a Chronology of Zuñi Ruins. *Anthropological Papers of the American Museum of Natural History,* Vol. 18, Part 3, pp. 207-331. New York.

1919   Ruins in the White Mountains, Arizona *Anthropological Papers of the American Museum of Natural History,* Vol. 18, Part 5, pp. 363-87. New York.

STUBBS, S. A. AND W. S. STALLINGS, JR.
1953   The Excavation of Pindi Pueblo, New Mexico. *Monographs of the School of American Research and the Laboratory of Anthropology,* No. 18. Santa Fe.

THOMPSON, R. H. (EDITOR)
1956   An Archaeological Approach to the Study of Cultural Stability. In "Seminars in American Archaeology: 1955," edited by Robert Wauchope, pp. 31-57. *Memoirs of the Society for American Archaeology,* No. 11. Salt Lake City.

VIVIAN, R. G.

1959   The Hubbard Site and Other Tri-Wall
        Structures in New Mexico and Col-
        orado. *National Park Service, Ar-
        chaeological Research Series,* No. 5.
        Washington.

WASLEY, W. W.

1952   The Late Pueblo Occupation at Point
        of Pines, East-Central Arizona. MS,
        master's thesis, University of Arizona,
        Tucson.

1959   Cultural Implications of Style Trends
        in Southwestern Prehistoric Pottery:
        Basketmaker III to Pueblo II in West
        Central New Mexico. Doctoral disser-
        tation, University of Arizona. Univer-
        sity Microfilms, Ann Arbor.

1960   Salvage Archaeology on Highway 66 in
        Eastern Arizona. *American Antiquity,*
        Vol. 26, No. 1, pp. 30-42. Salt Lake
        City.

WENDORF, FRED

1950   A Report on the Excavation of a Small
        Ruin Near Point of Pines, East Central
        Arizona. *University of Arizona Bulle-
        tin,* Vol. 21, No. 3, *Social Science
        Bulletin,* No. 19. Tucson.

1953   Archaeological Studies in the Petrified
        Forest National Monument. *Museum
        of Northern Arizona, Bulletin* 27.
        Flagstaff.

1956   The Ceramic Analysis. In *Pipeline
        Archaeology,* edited by Fred Wendorf,
        Nancy Fox, and O. L. Lewis, pp. 5-6.
        Laboratory of Anthropology and
        Museum of Northern Arizona, Santa
        Fe and Flagstaff.

WENDORF, FRED AND D. J. LEHMER

1956   Archaeology of the Wingate Products
        Line. In *Pipeline Archaeology,* edited
        by Fred Wendorf, Nancy Fox, and O.
        L. Lewis, pp. 158-95. Laboratory
        of Anthropology and Museum of
        Northern Arizona, Santa Fe and
        Flagstaff.

WHEAT, J. B.

1952   Prehistoric Water Sources of the Point
        of Pines Area. *American Antiquity,*
        Vol. 17, No. 3, pp. 185-96. Salt Lake
        City.

1955   Mogollon Culture Prior to A.D. 1000.
        *Memoirs of the Society for American
        Archaeology,* No. 10. Salt Lake City.

WHEAT, J. B., J. C. GIFFORD, AND W. W. WASLEY

1958   Ceramic Variety, Type Cluster, and
        Ceramic System in Southwestern
        Pottery Analysis. *American Antiquity,*
        Vol. 24, No. 1, pp. 34-47. Salt Lake
        City.

WOODBURY, RICHARD B. AND NATHALIE F. S.
        WOODBURY

1956   Zuni Prehistory and El Morro National
        Monument. *Southwestern Lore,* Vol.
        21, pp. 56-60. Boulder.

1966   Decorated Pottery of the Zuni Area.
        Appendix II in *Contributions From
        the Museum of the American Indian,
        Heye Foundation,* Vol. XX, by
        Watson Smith, R. B. Woodbury, and
        Nathalie F. S. Woodbury, New York.

ANTHROPOLOGICAL PAPERS OF THE UNIVERSITY OF ARIZONA

1. Excavations at Nantack Village, Point of Pines, Arizona. David A. Breternitz. 1959. (O.P.)
2. Yaqui Myths and Legends. Ruth W. Giddings. 1959. *Now in bock form.*
3. Marobavi: A Study of an Assimilated Group in Northern Sonora. Roger C. Owen. 1959. (O.P.)
4. A Survey of Indian Assimilation in Eastern Sonora. Thomas B. Hinton. 1959. (O.P.)
5. The Phonology of Arizona Yaqui with Texts. Lynn S. Crumrine. 1961. (O.P., D)
6. The Maricopas: An Identification from Documentary Sources. Paul H. Ezell. 1963. (O.P.)
7. The San Carlos Indian Cattle Industry. Harry T. Getty. 1964. (O.P.)
8. The House Cross of the Mayo Indians of Sonora, Mexico. N. Ross Crumrine. 1964. (O.P.)
9. Salvage Archaeology in Painted Rocks Reservoir, Western Arizona. William W. Wasley and Alfred E. Johnson. 1965.
10. An Appraisal of Tree-Ring Dated Pottery in the Southwest. David A. Breternitz. 1966. (O.P.)
11. The Albuquerque Navajos. William H. Hodge. 1969. (O.P.)
12. Papago Indians at Work. Jack O. Waddell. 1969.
13. Culture Change and Shifting Populations in Central Northern Mexico. William B. Griffen. 1969.
14. Ceremonial Exchange as a Mechanism in Tribal Integration Among the Mayos of Northwest Mexico. Lynn S. Crumrine. 1969. (O.P.)
15. Western Apache Witchcraft. Keith H. Basso. 1969.
16. Lithic Analysis and Cultural Inference: A Paleo-Indian Case. Edwin N. Wilmsen. 1970. (O.P.)
17. Archaeology as Anthropology: A Case Study. William A. Longacre. 1970.
18. Broken K Pueblo: Prehistoric Social Organization in the American Southwest. James N. Hill. 1970. (O.P., D)
19. White Mountain Redware: A Pottery Tradition of East-Central Arizona and Western New Mexico. Roy L. Carlson. 1970.
20. Mexican Macaws: Comparative Osteology. Lyndon L. Hargrave. 1970. (O.P.)
21. Apachean Culture History and Ethnology. Keith H. Basso and Morris E. Opler, eds. 1971.
22. Social Functions of Language in a Mexican-American Community. George C. Barker. 1972. (O.P.)
23. The Indians of Point of Pines, Arizona: A Comparative Study of Their Physical Characteristics. Kenneth A. Bennett. 1973. (O.P.)
24. Population, Contact, and Climate in the New Mexico Pueblos. Ezra B. W. Zubrow. 1974. (O.P.)
25. Irrigation's Impact on Society. Theodore E. Downing and McGuire Gibson, eds. 1974. (O.P.)
26. Excavations at Punta de Agua in the Santa Cruz River Basin, Southeastern Arizona. J. Cameron Greenleaf. 1975. (O.P.)
27. Seri Prehistory: The Archaeology of the Central Coast of Sonora, Mexico. Thomas Bowen. 1976. (O.P.)
28. Carib-Speaking Indians: Culture, Society, and Language. Ellen B. Basso, ed. 1977. (O.P.)
29. Cocopa Ethnography William H. Kelly. 1977. (O.P., D.)
30. The Hodges Ruin: A Hohokam Community in the Tucson Basin. Isabel Kelly, James E. Officer, and Emil W. Haury, collaborators; Gayle H. Hartmann, ed. 1978. (O.P.)
31. Fort Bowie Material Culture. Robert M. Herskovitz. 1978. (O.P.)
32. Artifacts from Chaco Canyon, New Mexico: The Chetro Ketl Collection. R. Gwinn Vivian, Dulce N. Dodgen, and Gayle H. Hartmann. 1978. (O.P.)
33. Indian Assimilation in the Franciscan Area of Nueva Vizcaya. William B. Griffen. 1979.
34. The Durango South Project: Archaeological Salvage of Two Late Basketmaker III Sites in the Durango District. John D. Gooding. 1980.
35. Basketmaker Caves in the Prayer Rock District, Northeastern Arizona. Elizabeth Ann Morris. 1980.
36. Archaeological Explorations in Caves of the Point of Pines Region, Arizona. James C. Gifford. 1980.
37. Ceramic Sequences in Colima: Capacha, an Early Phase. Isabel Kelly. 1980.
38. Themes of Indigenous Acculturation in Northwest Mexico. Thomas B. Hinton and Phil C. Weigand, eds. 1981.
39. Sixteenth Century Maiolica Pottery in the Valley of Mexico. Florence C. Lister and Robert H. Lister. 1982.
40. Multidisciplinary Research at Grasshopper Pueblo, Arizona. William A. Longacre, Sally J. Holbrook, and Michael W. Graves, eds. 1982.
41. The Asturian of Cantabria: Early Holocene Hunter-Gatherers in Northern Spain. Geoffrey A. Clark. 1983.
42. The Cochise Cultural Sequence in Southeastern Arizona. E. B. Sayles. 1983.
43. Cultural and Environmental History of Cienega Valley, Southeastern Arizona. Frank W. Eddy and Maurice E. Cooley. 1983.

44. Settlement, Subsistence, and Society in Late Zuni Prehistory.   Keith W. Kintigh. 1985. (O.P., D)

45. The Geoarchaeology of Whitewater Draw, Arizona.   Michael R. Waters. 1986.

46. Ejidos and Regions of Refuge in Northwestern Mexico.   N. Ross Crumrine and Phil C. Weigand, eds. 1987.

47. Preclassic Maya Pottery at Cuello, Belize.   Laura J. Kosakowsky. 1987.

48. Pre-Hispanic Occupance in the Valley of Sonora, Mexico.   William E. Doolittle. 1988.

49. Mortuary Practices and Social Differentiation at Casas Grandes, Chihuahua, Mexico.   John C. Ravesloot. 1988.

50. Point of Pines, Arizona: A History of the University of Arizona Archaeological Field School.   Emil W. Haury. 1989.

51. Patarata Pottery: Classic Period Ceramics of the South-central Gulf Coast, Veracruz, Mexico.   Barbara L. Stark. 1989.

52. The Chinese of Early Tucson: Historic Archaeology from the Tucson Urban Renewal Project.   Florence C. Lister and Robert H. Lister. 1989.

53. Mimbres Archaeology of the Upper Gila, New Mexico.   Stephen H. Lekson. 1990. (O.P.)

54. Prehistoric Households at Turkey Creek Pueblo, Arizona.   Julie C. Lowell. 1991.

55. Homol'ovi II: Archaeology of an Ancestral Hopi Village, Arizona.   E. Charles Adams and Kelley Ann Hays, eds. 1991. (O.P., D)

56. The Marana Community in the Hohokam World.   Suzanne K. Fish, Paul R. Fish, and John H. Madsen, eds. 1992.

57. Between Desert and River: Hohokam Settlement and Land Use in the Los Robles Community.   Christian E. Downum. 1993. (O.P., D)

58. Sourcing Prehistoric Ceramics at Chodistaas Pueblo, Arizona: The Circulation of People and Pots in the Grasshopper Region.   María Nieves Zedeño. 1994.

59. Of Marshes and Maize: Preceramic Agricultural Settlements in the Cienega Valley, Southeastern Arizona.   Bruce B. Huckell. 1995.

60. Historic Zuni Architecture and Society: An Archaeological Application of Space Syntax.   T. J. Ferguson. 1996.

61. Ceramic Commodities and Common Containers: Production and Distribution of White Mountain Red Ware in the Grasshopper Region, Arizona.   Daniela Triadan. 1997.

62. Prehistoric Sandals from Northeastern Arizona: The Earl H. Morris and Ann Axtell Morris Research.   Kelley Ann Hays-Gilpin, Ann Cordy Deegan, and Elizabeth Ann Morris. 1998.

63. Expanding the View of Hohokam Platform Mounds: An Ethnographic Perspective.   Mark D. Elson. 1998.

64. Great House Communities Across the Chacoan Landscape.   John Kantner and Nancy M. Mahoney, eds. 2000.

65. Tracking Prehistoric Migrations: Pueblo Settlers among the Tonto Basin Hohokam.   Jeffery J. Clark. 2001.

66. Beyond Chaco: Great Kiva Communities on the Mogollon Rim Frontier.   Sarah A. Herr. 2001.

67. Salado Archaeology of the Upper Gila, New Mexico.   Stephen H. Lekson. 2002.

68. Ancestral Hopi Migrations.   Patrick D. Lyons. 2003.

69. Ancient Maya Life in the Far West Bajo: Social and Environmental Change in the Wetlands of Belize.   Julie L. Kunen. 2004.

Anthropological Papers listed as O.P., D are available as Docutech reproductions (high quality xerox) printed on demand. They are tape or spiral bound and nonreturnable.